TRENDS IN
PROJECT MANAGEMENT

Volume 1

Thank You... Beatrix for your time. I hope you enjoy the book Michael D.

Quay
CONSULTING

Copyright @ 2015 Quay Consulting Pty Ltd

ISBN: 978-1-925341-74-4 (Print Edition)
Published by Vivid Publishing
P.O. Box 948, Fremantle
Western Australia 6959
www.vividpublishing.com.au

Quay Consulting
Level 9, 19-31 Pitt Street
Sydney NSW 2000
www.quayconsulting.com.au

Cataloguing-in-Publication data is available from the National Library of Australia

Subjects include: Project management, portfolio management, transformation, change management, architecture, systems integration, capability uplift, stakeholder management and testing management.

Acknowledgements

Quay Consulting is a professional services business operating in the project management landscape, transforming strategy into fit-for-purpose project delivery.

We published the first Quay Bulletin in September 2012 with the aim of providing our clients and industry with thought leadership around the principles of delivering better projects. Since then, we have built a library of articles that covers PMO, Architecture, Change Management, Project Management, Transformation and more.

This compilation brings that thought leadership together to help your team improve project delivery across your organisation.

With thanks to Rod Adams, Michael Bolton, Orla Kassis, Brad Kane, Marcel Thompson, Pramod Goel and Rebecca Bennett for their contributions to this book.

For more information about Quay Consulting, visit www.quayconsulting.com.au

Chapters

CHAPTER 1 - TO THE CLOUD

CHAPTER 2 - AGILE, WATERFALL OR HYBRID

CHAPTER 3 - DEVELOPING BETTER PROJECT MANAGERS

CHAPTER 4 - DEVELOPING BETTER PROJECT SPONSORS

CHAPTER 5 - HOW TO TRANSFORM

CHAPTER 6 - PMOS: THE HOWS AND THE WHYS

CHAPTER 7 - MANAGING ORGANISATIONAL CHANGE

CHAPTER 8 - THE RISE OF BIG DATA & DIGITAL

CHAPTER 9 - WHY GOVERNANCE IS ALWAYS THE KEY

CHAPTER 10 - PROJECT MANAGEMENT: THE THINGS THEY DON'T TEACH YOU AT SCHOOL

CHAPTER 11 - WHEN IN DOUBT, PLAN

CHAPTER 12 - STRATEGY & ARCHITECTURE: KEY ENABLERS TO SUCCESS

CHAPTER 1
TO THE CLOUD!

How are Cloud projects different?

Without doubt Cloud technology is the latest trend being embraced by organisations to manage their infrastructure (IaaS), applications (SaaS), and development platform (PaaS).

It is a trend that will only gather pace over the coming years as increasing pressure is brought upon IT budgets across all industries and Cloud delivery and costs models mature. An argument in favour of cloud assets is the ability to shrink the IT footprint and transfer commodity services to others whilst keeping your specialist skills in-house.

For example, your development and deployment environments may be delivered via PaaS, but the development expertise stays within your internal teams. As a result, organisations are increasingly looking for project managers who have experience in delivering Cloud projects.

But do Cloud projects require new techniques or specific expertise or can the tried and tested approaches to project delivery be readily translated to Cloud projects?

Transfer of technology, retention of knowledge

The industry-accepted definition of Cloud Computing is the delivery of infrastructure, application and data services to organisations using the Internet as the network.

The management and security of the IT platform and services is essentially outsourced to 3rd parties with the physical sites being remote or 'in the cloud'. A Cloud solution can therefore be a series of moving parts across infrastructure, networks, applications, data and outsourcing.

From a project delivery perspective, the key components of a Cloud project are well known and would be nothing new to an experienced project manager.

It is however the blend of the solution and heightened importance of some of these elements that set a Cloud project apart from a traditional Infrastructure or Application project.

These include:

1. A greater focus is required on change and stakeholder management around security of data

Whether fact or fiction business will become nervous with the thought that their data will now be stored off site and managed by a third party and is therefore at greater risk of compromise.

Project managers delivering Cloud projects need to take this into account and ensure their testing cycles are fit for purpose and the management of stakeholder expectations is given priority to adequately address heightened concerns around data security.

2. By using the Internet, the network access takes on greater importance

Project managers need to ensure the internal and external gateways are reliable, secure and well supported and can cope with the expected increases in data heading in both directions.

3. Service Delivery Models

SLAs and the service delivery model need to be both very well understood and steps taken to test and ensure that they are fit for purpose.

With the support being largely outsourced for the cloud component it is imperative that stakeholders are comfortable the SLAs will meet the needs of the business in terms of business continuity and support and the IT organisation knows who is on point for addressing an issue no matter where it occurs in the end to end business process.

4. Understanding total cost of project takes on added importance during the business case phase

Cloud solutions can be cost effective to set up but may become very expensive once operational due to the common use of transactional costs models. It is important these BAU operational costs are accurately modeled and clearly understood and communicated to stakeholders for approval.

Cloud projects are set to become more prevalent over the next decade if current industry trends continue.

By following some of the above steps project managers should be better equipped to understand what makes a Cloud project unique and therefore take suitable actions to ensure their projects are set up for success.

What are the benefits of the cloud?

Organisations should seek to justify the project investment before embarking on a cloud project by identifying and quantifying the benefits.

There is without doubt a growing trend for organisations to leverage cloud-based solutions, with three options to choose from when deciding which model to adopt – public, private or a hybrid cloud combining elements of both public and private.

Despite the growing trend, organisations should still seek to justify the project investment before embarking on a cloud project by identifying and quantifying the benefits.

Like most change initiatives, the benefits for cloud are a combination of the tangible and intangible. Below is a list of the most compelling benefits that are emerging for organisations that are driving the rapid adoption of cloud solutions.

Ease of use

By pooling resources and better configuration, cloud service providers can deliver a greatly enhanced user experience by increasing the ease of use of applications and services.

The reasons for the increase in ease of use can include more remote access options with enhanced reliability and support, increased self-service opportunities and increases in speed of delivery.

Pay as you go models

Cloud solutions can remove the need for large investment in infrastructure up front. This enables cloud providers to offer pay as you go transactional models to organisations. These models can deliver real savings to organisations as they are only billed for what they use.

Virtual infrastructure that is highly scalable

When adopting cloud solutions organisations can essentially outsource both their infrastructure and applications layers.

By moving these things into the cloud organisations can not only reduce replacement, maintenance and support costs but also take advantage of highly scalable, non static IT environments.

Reduced complexity of IT environments

It would be incorrect to say cloud environments are not complex; they are however a large portion of this complexity is outsourced to the Cloud provider.

But by leveraging cloud solutions, particularly public cloud solutions, the need to manage these complex environments is transferred from the organisation's IT department to the cloud service providers.

Reduce the cost of customisation

Whilst cloud platforms often allow a customised development opportunity for the user, the core of the cloud service is standardised and quarantined from this customised layer.

This separation enables upgrades to the core service without impacting the customisations. Unlike in-house IT managed platforms where heavily intertwined layers mean upgrades can be costly and time consuming.

Data storage

The cloud can be leveraged to store an organisation's data by replacing existing on-site data storage facilities like data centres. This can enable organisations to decommission costly storage facilities and only pay for the data they actually need to store.

Ultimately the benefits of any new solution must be weighed against the risks, costs and other relevant factors in play for the organisation.

It is important for organisations to resist simply following the latest trends for the sake of it. This is no different when considering the use of the cloud.

Organisations should continue to deploy good project disciplines by ensuring the benefits are fully researched and understood up front before embarking upon any change.

What should you migrate into the cloud?

Migrating into the cloud is the subject du jour. But what systems should you take online?

A quick scan of many business and IT conversations in the digital world often focus on moving traditionally server-based or in-house systems out-of-house and into the cloud.

Many of the arguments for – and against – cloud services are challenged by the reality that every business has its own unique operating model that must factor its ability to leverage staff and IT environments to take advantage of its unique competitive advantage.

What is increasingly becoming a clear and valid argument is that the cloud offers a viable choice to migrate or shift to cloud-based technology, environments and applications to support business capabilities.

So how do we determine what makes sense to be in the cloud?

The obvious contenders

There are many views as to the 'obvious' targets for moving into a cloud environment: email, servers and CRM as well as development environments which provide simplicity and speed-to-scale on demand without the upfront investment of owning assets in-house.

It's the information and unique value proposition of a business that wins revenue and in most instances, the above applications do not provide any real competitive advantage which makes them good candidates to move to the cloud.

The complex contenders

Where bespoke (normally developed in-house) applications are in use the decision to migrate to the cloud creates an additional layer of complexity.

In this instance careful consideration should be given to whether or not the application could be migrated to the cloud (in effect hosted), replaced with a SaaS application providing similar functionality or left in house.

The costs to migrate are not insignificant and extend beyond the application to include other costs such as change management (where an application is replaced this normally includes business process re-engineering as well).

Risk + ROI + implementation + business case

As security and network infrastructure has matured there are fewer barriers to migrating into the cloud. It is Quay's view, shared by a number of our clients, that each technology, application or environment has provision by way of the cloud as an option.

From a strategy perspective a cloud-based solution should always be an option considered against others looking at risk, return on investment, ease of implementation and time to implement.

The decision of whether or not to migrate to the cloud should be done in the context of a business case with all solutions and options coming under consideration.

Sometimes the cloud will be the best outcome, others not – this is very situational and each case should be assessed on it's own merits.

The cloud is a mechanism, not a process

Whatever the outcome remember the cloud is just a mechanism to provide tools for the business. The end-to-end business processes will need to still work which may involve multiple cloud assets working with in house assets.

Careful investigation should be given as to the extent to which the technologies and processes can seamlessly integrated and the SLAs around that and furthermore how customisations can occur independently of the cloud asset.

A final thought. When you migrate to the cloud ensure you have the vendor management skills in-house to manage your cloud vendors. They will now become key partners to your business and need to be managed accordingly.

So the answer to what makes sense to migrate to the cloud will be found by applying some guiding principles and looking at each opportunity on its merits. The cloud is certainly becoming an increasingly trusted method to provide applications, infrastructure and platforms and should be considered for your business.

Cloud models: Not a 'one-size-fits-all'

What are the pros and cons of public, private and hybrid cloud solutions and which one is right for your organisation?

Moving into the Cloud is increasingly being seen as an important consideration when reviewing how IT supports and delivers services within the business, but like many things, it is not a one-size-fits-all equation.

There is a lot of confusion about which Cloud options are available and which will be most suitable for the business.

However, there are several ways to configure Cloud solutions for business and we explore the pros and cons of the three most common Cloud options: Public, Private and Hybrid.

But first, let's define what is meant by "the Cloud".

The Cloud: A definition

In a textbook sense, the Cloud is the delivery of computing as a service where shared resources, software, and information is provided to computers and other devices as a utility usually accessed via the Internet.

The Cloud provides large pools of resources connected via networks that allow on demand scalability for infrastructure, applications, data and storage enabling rapid scale and deployment opportunities. So how does this differ for private, public and hybrid Cloud configurations?

Public Clouds

Public Clouds are owned and operated by independent third-party service providers, typically large in scale and are offered to the public on a user pays model.

All users share the same infrastructure, for example Dropbox. Public Cloud services in general are targeted to individuals and organisations that do not require high levels of security, systems integration or data privacy.

The primary benefit of the Public Cloud is the provision of this access to resources and sophisticated technology for a fraction of the purchase price.

Furthermore, Public Clouds provide almost unlimited scalability allowing their services to be effectively "procured on-demand".

The main downside to the Public Cloud is the perception of the security of data in a shared environment. For some businesses the specification of where data is held being determined by the service provider; in some instances this could be offshore, which may result in potential issues for privacy and compliance.

There is however a counter argument that the services providers spend millions of dollars to ensure your security and privacy and may in fact be more secure than private enterprise.

Private Clouds

Private Clouds are built exclusively for an organisation, allowing it to operate in a cloud environment. There are two main types of Private Cloud: On-Site and External.

On-site, as the name suggests, means the resources are hosted within the organisations own premises (data centre).

External means the resources are built for the organisation exclusively but provided by an external provider.

The primary benefit of the Private Cloud is that is provides technology as a virtualised service to the organisation without the same privacy concerns of the Public Cloud.

Private Clouds offer scope for advanced security, high availability and fault tolerances that may not be available in Public Cloud offerings.

It also allows you to control precisely where data and information is held to ensure compliance and privacy regulations are met.

The downside of Private Clouds is that they require a significant capital investment and as such are not procured on demand like the Public Cloud.

Due to the significant investment required the scalability is limited to the investment made – which in almost all cases will be significantly less than the Public Cloud offerings.

Hybrid Clouds

Hybrid Clouds, which are becoming increasingly popular, comprise a combination of both Public and Private Cloud offerings.

In a Hybrid Cloud model, an organisation can leverage third party Cloud offerings whether in full or partially depending upon their specific requirements.

Augmenting a traditional Private Cloud with the resources of a Public Cloud can help manage temporary spikes in load without the investment required to meet the demand of a Private Cloud environment.

The main benefit of the Hybrid model is that it allows the organisation to have the best of both options depending upon its requirements.

An organisation can steer certain data and information to a Private Cloud to ensure security and compliance measures are satisfied whilst leveraging the scalability of the Public Cloud for load.

The downside of the hybrid model is complexity. Implementing a hybrid model requires diligent requirement gathering, skilful set-up and management, which comes at an additional cost, both in terms of technology and effort.

Understand your business and service level requirements

No matter which Cloud option or options your business leverages it is important to remember that the Cloud at its best offers a way to have technology provided in a more cost effective or efficient way. But it can mean added complexity of support.

Another thing to be mindful of: where non-production systems and production systems differ (i.e. private vs public Cloud), your environments also differ. Your testing needs to reflect this as well as any non-functional requirements such as configuration, storage, latency and disaster recovery.

Be sure to understand what your service level requirements are and that your service providers can support those requirements.

Cloud data security: Managing business risk

Data Security is a material consideration for a business when assessing which cloud model is the best fit for your organisation. There are generally three recognised cloud models: public, private and hybrid clouds.

In our August bulletin, we looked at the pros and cons that these cloud models offered a business, such as cost savings and improved outcomes for individuals and organisations.

This month, we look at what a business should understand about assessing and mitigating risks of moving into the cloud in particular when considering Data Security

Assessing the risks

Regardless of the model security of data is a material consideration across all three Cloud variations when deciding which model is the best for for your organisation. When assessing the risks to data in the Cloud it will vary depending on a number of factors.

These factors include:

- The sensitivity of the data to be stored or processed
- The criticality of the business process and
- How the chosen Cloud service provider has implemented their specific cloud services.

Quay recommends adopting a risk-based approach to deciding how the Cloud fits into your business, and we explore below some key considerations when making your Cloud decisions.

Maintaining availability and business functionality

Maintaining availability and business functionality must be looked at in the context of what your business needs to operate, in particular:

Consideration should be given to Service Level Agreements, what the vendor's disaster recovery plan is for both system and data availability and how this works in practice.

Understanding the physical location, network connectivity, data storage and physical infrastructure for both live and back-up data.

These are important considerations when assessing whether or not you feel the solution you are planning to implement is robust and secure enough to not put your critical data and processes at risk in the event of a failure.

Protection of your data from unauthorised access by a third party

Brute-force attacks and intrusion by a third party is a vital consideration when choosing your organisation's cloud model.

It's important to understand the pros and cons of a less secure public cloud through to the most secure private cloud option to gain insight into the cost and benefits of securing your data.

Consideration should also be given to:

- The sensitivity of the data
- Legislative requirements
- Physical location where the data is stored and
- The local laws regarding access and the applications of encryption technologies.

You might even find that the public cloud may have stronger data protection than you can afford under a hybrid or private cloud model.

However, it's not just about securing the data from unwanted attacks and access from 3rd parties.

Consideration should also be given to where a hybrid cloud is used (or a shared private cloud) as to what limitations are in place to prevent access to the data from others sharing the cloud and even the vendor's employees.

Are sufficient incident management protocols in place?

There is another critical area we believe worthy of mention and it focusses on process. Where multiple IT services operate to provide the business service, you need to ensure that each IT component has the appropriate SLA in place to meet your requirements.

Where vendors are involved, there are several points to investigate as part of your decision making process, for example:

- The systems they use
- Evidence of their actual response and resolution times and
- Their business continuity plans are all worthy of investigation.
- Any touch points or hand over points that may slip between the cracks in terms of support during an incident.

Often it is how vendors respond when things go wrong that is the true measure of the quality of the service they are providing.

Understand the implications for risk, compliance and continuity

The decision to move to the cloud is not just about having scalable infrastructure or software as a service.

There also needs to be due consideration of the processes and information being shifted and the implications from a risk, compliance and business continuity perspective to ensure the right mix for your business is achieved and your data remains as secure as possible.

The value proposition of ERP in the cloud

In making the case for traditional vs cloud ERP: what is the business case for transitioning to the cloud?

Many organisations are being challenged by the development of agile approaches to project delivery and an increasingly dynamic business environment dominated by quick turnaround digital challenges, often struggling to justify the business case for implementing traditional Enterprise Resource Planning (ERP) solutions.

By 'traditional', we infer an ERP that is purchased, developed with bespoke configuration, installed on local hardware and supported by an on-site IT team.

The traditional ERP remains a very powerful business enablement system but the business case does have several shortcomings, not least of which is that these projects are slow in terms of speed to implement due to the complexity.

Traditional ERPs are also costly as the full system must often be implemented and supported even if only a limited amount of the system functionality will be used initially.

Cloud-based models such as Software-as-a-Service (SaaS), however, have the potential to deliver the benefits of a traditional ERP without the downsides.

Integration, ownership costs, performance and accessibility, upgrade paths and speed to deploy are just some of the issues an organisation must address when deciding how to implement an ERP that is most suitable for their business.

In this article, we'll analyse the various considerations that should be undertaken when evaluating the implementation of traditional, on-site ERP vs a cloud-based ERP.

Integration – can we quickly integrate other systems with our ERP?

Integration is a vital consideration for a chosen ERP solution, particularly given the speed with which organisations need to react to new technology platforms to interact with customers and that much of that interaction happens in the digital space.

Potentially, cloud-based systems have an advantage here. Whilst it may seem counter-intuitive, the right cloud-based providers will already be fielding queries from multiple customers about how to integrate many different systems and tools that meet changing business needs.

Cloud-based ERP providers know that they need to provide enhanced services, so they could already be doing your R&D for you.

Cost of ownership – what is your investment

Cost of ownership is a significant factor in ERP solutions.

Traditional ERP systems that live onsite require a large, upfront spend to purchase, implement and manage software, hardware and other facilities necessary to run them, including suitably skilled IT staff.

Additionally, there is a significant ongoing cost to ensure systems are constantly up and running to meet BAU requirements and future upgrade costs.

With Cloud-based ERP solutions, the value proposition is often better. The upfront implementation costs are generally much lower as it is only a configuration exercise, rather than full deployment.

Secondly, the service provider hosts and maintains the IT infrastructure, is responsible for ensuring system availability, data security and future upgrades.

The cloud approach is typically a 'pay as you go' subscription model so you are only charged for the functionality and bandwidth you use, which makes the cloud based model potentially more financially attractive.

Reliability – System performance and accessibility

Cloud-based service providers can exceed performance and accessibility KPIs as they have greater resources to invest in hardware and bandwidth than individual organisations due to their one-to-many model.

But the key here is if you decide to go for a cloud-based ERP, then you must choose your service provider wisely and ensure they have a very good track record in providing fast and reliable access. SLAs will be a critical consideration.

Future scope – Enhancements and future upgrades

The traditional vs cloud-based approach probably cancel themselves out here. The core issue is the amount of configuration (read "customisation") that you drive into either system. The further you move away from the vanilla-flavoured model the greater the cost in terms of time and money required for future upgrades and enhancements.

Cloud-based ERP solutions probably have a slight advantage here, as typically they will not allow unlimited customisations during implementation. In effect this approach protects organisations from themselves and limits the complexity of the solution.

Speed to deploy

Cloud-based ERP solutions usually are much quicker to deploy, as it is more a configuration exercise than a traditional system deployment. There is no need to purchase and install hardware and train staff in the maintenance of the devices and systems. A cloud-based ERP solution simply needs an Internet connection and a set of robust requirements and the service provider can take it from there.

Cloud ERP: A viable alternative

Whilst there are other issues when deciding what type of ERP platform suits your organisation the analysis above highlights some of the more prominent considerations that need to be taken into account.

The rise of cloud-based ERP options should be taken for what it is, another possible solution to meeting your organisations ERP requirements, and should always be a consideration to the traditional on-site ERP.

Cloud Projects: Infrastructure Projects in Disguise?

Are cloud projects that much different to traditional infrastructure projects? What are the knowledge gaps that project managers need to be aware of?

Increasingly organisations are taking to the Cloud to manage their infrastructure (IaaS), applications (SaaS), and development platforms (PaaS).

It's a trend that is set to continue as organisations look to simply their IT platforms and drive efficiencies and savings.

The transition to Cloud-based solutions is leading to an increased demand for project managers with Cloud delivery expertise.

But are Cloud projects that much different to traditional Infrastructure projects and what are the knowledge gaps if any that a project manager needs to be aware of?

The crossover between traditional and cloud infrastructure

Firstly, it depends on what type of Cloud solution the organisation is implementing.

There are three widely accepted cloud models; public, private or a hybrid cloud combining elements of both public and private. Each has their own unique requirements and challenges.

However, all still retain significant crossovers with traditional Infrastructure Projects. Below we have identified some of the unique challenges project managers need to be cognisant of when delivering a Cloud project as opposed to a traditional Infrastructure Project.

Data Access

Key data will now potentially be stored off-site. Cloud-based data access requires that additional steps must be taken during the project to test that the data will be accessible according to the agreed SLAs and data accuracy.

This additional focus could include greater volume testing, testing for remote access and understanding the Cloud service providers break/fix process when key data is not available.

Security

With Cloud solutions applications and data could now be stored physically off-site in new or yet to be tested production environments provided by the Cloud service provider.

The project manager should take extra steps to ensure the locations are secure and meet the organisations security SLAs.

Integration

Particularly with Hybrid Cloud models there is a greater complexity in the Solution Architecture, often with a mix and match of where the various components (application, infrastructure, data etc) physically reside and who is responsible for them.

The Project Manager needs to be aware of this greater complexity and plan accordingly around delivery and testing the various integration points between the organisations systems and platforms and those of the Cloud service provider.

People Management

During Cloud implementations much of the delivery team will be off-site, in multiple locations and potentially overseas in different time zones.

Project managers should be mindful of these additional vendor management requirements and plan the project governance and communications accordingly and look to use effective meeting technology (i.e. Skype) where appropriate.

Escalations

With the reliance on external solution providers instead of in-house teams the path to escalate issues will be significantly different.

Project managers need to be much more aware of what are the paths for escalation and make sure they are fit for purpose to ensure issues can be readily triaged and fixed in suitable time frames regardless of the reporting lines or location of the various teams.

The Cloud Infrastructure Checklist

Whilst Cloud projects share many characteristics with traditional Infrastructure projects there are some significant differences.

Whilst the above list is not exhaustive it is a sound starting checklist for use by a project manager who may be embarking on their first Cloud project and if followed should help set them up for success.

CHAPTER 2

AGILE, WATERFALL OR HYBRID?

When is Agile the right approach?

Agile can be a very effective project delivery methodology when it is executed correctly.

The first challenge is not how to deliver a project successfully in an Agile way but to assess when the use of Agile is most appropriate.

Not one-size-fits-all

Agile can drive significant rewards by increasing the speed of delivery and benefit realisation by consistently targeting those requirements within a project that will deliver the greatest benefits, however it is not a one-size-fits-all approach.

An Agile approach attempts to reduce inherent project risk by embedding the business in the team and breaking a project into smaller segments, providing more ease-of-change during the development process. A key emphasis is on fulfilling the business need via speedy delivery and low cost, whilst technological or engineering excellence is generally of lesser importance.

The aim is to produce high quality systems quickly, primarily through the use of iterative prototyping, active user involvement, and computerised development tools.

When is Agile most successful?

In Quay's experience for Agile techniques to be successful there needs to be a certain set of circumstances present within the organisation as well as a thorough understanding of the type of project being embarked upon.

To help make this assessment Quay has developed the following checklists to help organisations when they are considering the use of Agile.

These checklists can be played back against an organisation's business case, risk profile, current delivery capability and the nature of the project to assess if Agile is the optimal approach.

The first checklist concentrates on Agile's key strengths and weaknesses in comparison to the more traditional Waterfall or Iterative approaches to project delivery:

Agile Strengths

- The operational version of an application is available much earlier
- Produces more business focussed outcomes at a lower cost
- Greater level of commitment and ownership from business and technical stakeholders
- Produces a tighter fit between user requirements and system specifications
- Concentrates on essential system elements from user viewpoint and provides the ability to rapidly change system design as demanded by users

Agile Weaknesses

- May lead to lower overall system quality and scalability issues due to inconsistent designs within and across systems
- High cost of commitment required on the part of key user personnel, especially the business 'A' team
- Project may end up with more requirements than needed due to 'gold-plating'
- Risk of difficult problems to be pushed to the future to demonstrate early success to management
- Potential for violation of programming standards, inconsistent naming conventions, inconsistent documentation and lack of attention to later system administration needs

Once it is determined Agile would fit within an organisation the next step is to assess if Agile is suitable for delivering the specific project.

The checklist below identifies the key characteristics a project needs to lend itself to an Agile approach.

Where most appropriate to use Agile for a project

- Project is of small-to-medium scale and of short duration and application not infrastructure based
- Project scope is focused, such that the business objectives are well defined and narrow
- Users possess detailed knowledge of the application area and Senior management commitment exists to ensure end-user involvement
- It is not possible to define requirements accurately ahead of time because the situation is new or the system being employed is highly innovative
- Team composition is stable; continuity of core development team can be maintained
- Technical architecture is clearly defined and key technical components are in place and tested
- Development team is empowered to make design decisions on a day-to-day basis without the need for consultation with their superiors, and decisions can be made by a small number of people who are available and preferably co-located

Where least appropriate to use Agile for a project

- Large infrastructure projects, such as corporate-wide databases or real-time or safety-critical systems
- Systems where complex and voluminous data must be analysed, designed, and created
- Project scope is broad and the business objectives are obscure
- Applications where the functional requirements have to be fully specified before any programming
- Many people must be involved in the decisions on the project, and the decision makers are not available on a timely basis or they are geographically dispersed or disengaged
- Large project team or multiple teams whose work needs to be coordinated
- Many new technologies are to be introduced within the scope of the project, or the technical architecture is unclear and

much of the technology will be used for the first time within the project

The above checklists are not exhaustive and will not guarantee a successful Agile delivery.

However, they will assist in ensuring the project delivery approach selected, be it Agile or not, has been given due consideration, is fit for purpose and the project is set up for success as best as possible before it commences.

Can you fix the price on Agile projects?

Two trends are emerging in project delivery that may, on the surface at least, appear to be quite contradictory.

Many organisations are looking at ways to share project risk and quantify costs upfront by locking in fixed price contracts for project delivery at the same time as exploring Agile techniques for more rapid and targeted application development.

But can these two trends – fixed price project delivery and Agile co-exist or are they in fact mutually exclusive?

The hallmarks of fixed pricing vs an agile approach

Typically fixed pricing of projects has been the domain of waterfall methodologies whereby the scope, deliverables, governance and sequencing are understood and agreed up front. The vendor or project delivery organisation will include a premium in the fixed price in return for accepting the risk of owning the success or otherwise of the delivery of the project within the agreed constraints.

The hallmarks are the outcomes and benefits of the project are largely understood and agreed before work commences, the governance framework is robust and a traditional waterfall approach to the project delivery is used.

Agile projects operate in a more flexible and collaborative way. Agile does not have a signed-off scope instead a feature log is agreed and regular meetings are held (as frequently as weekly) with the customer to assess progress and adjust priorities as required.

The outcomes are less understood up front but in return the organisation is provided a delivery platform that is iterative and focused on speed to market and targeting the must have business functionality during the development life cycle.

The right circumstances for co-existence

Whilst the nature of Agile projects would seem at odds with a fixed price model, it is achievable given certain circumstances.

Firstly, the customer must have some clear view on the key functionality required and the order of importance.

This should be discussed, sanity-checked and scoped with the delivery team and will form the basis of the initial fixed price quote for effort to complete. This is then drawn down upon during execution.

A fixed price however should not be written in stone. One of the key benefits for an organisation when deploying Agile techniques is the ability to make quick business-focused decisions to re-prioritise what should be worked upon at any given point.

To enable fixed price costing and Agile to co-exist it is imperative there is a simple yet effective change control mechanism in place which allows for the effort to be re-directed as required and signed off in a timely and effective manner.

Equally it is critical that the communication between the delivery team and the customer is open and transparent.

Budget and spend checkpoints

There needs to be regular checkpoints of where the overall spend is up to and why, reconciling the initial scope with any change requests.

The delivery team must at all times work on the 'no surprises' principle and be very transparent on estimated costs, effort to date and where under-estimation is likely to occur.

Ultimately the trend toward customers expecting more accurate costing and the sharing of risk is a trend that is set to continue.

Whilst fixed pricing is not the ideal model for Agile techniques they are not mutually exclusive if there is a spirit of transparency, co-operation and flexibility on both sides to achieve the best outcomes.

How to select Agile over other methodologies

In the age of Agile, how can a simple decision making framework to ensure it is the most valid approach for upcoming projects?

Many organisations in their efforts to improve their project capability are turning to Agile as an alternate project delivery methodology to the traditional waterfall or iterative approaches.

Agile calls for less documentation and has certain advantages over other methodologies, particularly with real time application projects, but is not necessarily the best fit for all types of projects.

So to get the best results from Agile adoption, organisations are faced with the challenge of how to decide when it is the right time to adopt Agile over the usual waterfall and iterative approaches.

Create a Project Delivery Decision Making Framework

Agile is not always the most appropriate project delivery methodology and there should always be room to use alternate approaches as required.

If an organisation uses more than one methodology it is critical to develop a project delivery decision-making framework.

This decision-making framework should be used to assess and score a new project against agreed criteria to determine the most appropriate methodology to adopt to deliver the project: be it Agile, Waterfall or Iterative.

The table below represents a decision-making framework to select an appropriate methodology in simplistic terms. In reality the choice will be a more nuanced as a result of considered judgment of business representatives in collaboration with the delivery teams.

Agile Project	Iterative Project	Waterfall Project
Low business criticality	High business criticality	High business or safety critical system
Requirements change often/ not easy to define	Requirements are not easy to define or may be subject to change	Requirements are clear and stable over the development timeframe
Very low architecture and integration risks e.g. web applications	Low architecture and integration risks e.g. web information systems and event driven systems	Architecture and integration risks are high e.g. infrastructure or large mainframe project
Flexible governance and development requirements	Strong governance and development standards and requirements	Strong governance and development standards and requirements
Small number of developers	Large number of developers	Large number of developers
Senior experienced developers	Less experienced developers	Less experienced developers
Co-location of developers and stakeholders	Distributed teams	Distributed teams
Culture that thrives on change	Culture that demands order	Culture that demands order

Will there be different documentation produced?

Regardless of the approach adopted the generation of project documentation is a key consideration (what, when, sign off protocols etc.).

A general principal driving the adoption of Agile is it is documentation light and is an approach that can accept greater risk during delivery.

Developers only produce the necessary document, which during development is minimal because development cycles are short and the team is stable, cohesive and trusted. Iterative and waterfall approaches assume that interim documentation is necessary to cope with longer cycle time and personnel churn and the management of greater risk.

Whichever approach is adopted, we suggest any decision making framework should also define the most complete suite of documentation and indicate the primary purpose and consumer of each documentation item.

Plans at the project level would then indicate and justify which documents were not applicable to achieve balance and flexibility the framework should ensure that business and operations endorse the deletion of a documentation item for a particular project.

The growth of Agile

The adoption of Agile approaches to project delivery is only set to increase as organisations driven by commercial imperatives look to ramp up their ability to execute projects in a more timely manner.

The creation and adoption of a simple decision making framework is imperative for any organisation to ensure they have a checkpoint to assess when Agile is a most valid approach to use for an upcoming project.

CHAPTER 3

DEVELOPING BETTER PROJECT MANAGERS

Selecting the right project manager

If project management certification isn't the only consideration in choosing a project manager, what else should you look for?

Project management certification is usually a key consideration for many businesses in selecting a project manager, however certification isn't a guarantee of a good project manager. But what is? The answer: it depends.

Gaining certification

Project managers undertake both a written examination (normally multiple choice) and in some cases an evidence-based examination of previous work they've performed.

This is designed to test the project manager's recall ability of best practice as well as their documentation and organisation skills.

Whilst very valuable from an organisational and theoretical perspective the examination process has its limitations. In particular certification provides no insight into whether the project manager is the right cultural fit for the organisation and it also it fails to adequately address the single most important skill of a project manager – communication.

Experience at the coalface

Be it stakeholder management or team leadership, a project manager will need to spend up to 90% of their time communicating and leading to be effective.

Quay's experience has shown that more emphasis should be placed on stakeholder management skills and how the project manager fits with the organisation's internal culture than the certification they have gained.

Whilst certification is useful, there is little substitute for the battle scars of a seasoned project manager who has solid experience dealing with the issues and communication requirements of managing the many layers within an array of projects.

Assess the expertise and demonstrated experience

If certification isn't the only consideration, what else should be taken into account when selecting a PM for your project? At Quay, we look for demonstrated experience in:

- *Mature vs immature sponsor* - The maturity of the project's sponsor is an important factor in choosing the right project management expertise. An immature sponsor will need an experienced project manager who is very good at managing up to help guide them on how to be effective in their role.
- *Technical solutioning rather than managing* - Our experience has show that technical domain specialists can become side-tracked into solutioning and lose sight of managing the project. It is therefore important they are first and foremost well rounded project managers.
- *Methodology* - Are you implementing an agile, iterative or waterfall project? Make sure your Project Manager is competent in the approach to your project.
- *Application vs. Infrastructure* - Is the project more weighted to one than the other and if so does the project manager have the required experience in the domain?
- *IT vs. Business Project Management:* IT Project Managers understand the technology domain and its complexities but can be exposed on the business-centric projects where subject matter expertise and the ability to deal direct with the business is a key enabler of success.
- *PM making decisions rather than PM seeking decisions* - Stakeholder decision-making is a vital component of successful project delivery. Your project is likely to hit trouble if your project manager is making the key project decisions instead of the right stakeholder.

- *Certification should be part of the process – not the deciding factor -* Choosing a project manager with the appropriate skills for your project is an essential part of successful delivery.

Experience matters

As we have explored above, it is the experience that a project manager brings to a project that will determine how effectively they are able to bring stakeholders and team members on the project journey from scope to full implementation.

Whilst beneficial certification alone is not enough to ensure you choose the best person to manage your projects.

Distinguishing the roles of Project and Program Managers

What are the additional/new skills required to step up from a project manager to a program manager role?

As the profession of Project Management continues to evolve and mature the distinction between Project and Program Management is receiving more focus, attention and debate.

The PMI and AIPM have formalised the distinction in their communities by creating separate Project and Program Management credentials with program management focused on the competency to oversee multiple, related projects and their resources to achieve strategic business goals.

But when the rubber hits the road is this distinction by aggregation enough?

Management by Context

The practitioner in Quay believes that the major difference between Program and Project Management is less about how many project managers are reporting to a program manager and the dependencies and resources and more about the lens by which the Manager looks at the work being performed i.e. management by context.

The project manager will have defined scope, schedule, budget, work products, and outcomes – best practice sees these clearly articulated and agreed to by the appropriate governance.

The project manager will drive the process groups for each phase of the project such as initiation, planning, executing, monitoring, controlling and closing usually following some structured approach or methodology.

The program manager however has a different focus. A program manager is less about the PM101s and more about the return on investment and strategic alignment of the work being performed within their programs.

Holistic perspective, engagement and alignment

The program manager becomes a de facto business unit overseeing the execution of significant change to realise strategy.

The program manager thereby assumes a senior manager role in the organisation and accordingly must be equipped to understand the business holistically, engage and lead meaningful conversations with other leaders across the organisation and balance the competing demands of project managers (or stream leads) within their programs as well as the interests of the organisation as a whole (which at times will conflict).

Of course a solid knowledge of the PM101s and application of fit for purpose assurance measures across the project managers is a part of the program managers remit which can often be executed by a program management office rather than the program manager directly.

Managing the competing demands of projects within programs

Another key success factor for a program manager is the ability to apply reasoned judgment and particularly regarding the timing of when decisions need to be made or problems solved.

It is a reality that what is in the best interests of a project may not always be in the best interests of the program at large and the ability to balance these competing demands whilst keeping your teams enthused and focused on their project outcomes requires careful judgment, communication and sensitivity.

View program managers through a different lens

To summarise, the lens of project management is specific, structured and managed through process whereas the lens of program management is contextual, less structured and management through executive leadership.

So when selecting your program manager make sure you look carefully at their EQ and ensure you have selected an executive leader capable of addressing the challenges that lie ahead.

Successfully mentoring new project managers within your organisation

How can you best develop, mentor and support new project managers in your organisation?

One of the key challenges many organisations face is developing in-house project delivery capability whilst continuing to maintain a successful operation. New project managers pose a quandary: at some point a new project manager must be developed and brought up through the ranks yet few sponsors want a 'developing' project manager in charge of delivering their projects.

Whilst most sponsors want an experienced project manager on their project, businesses who take the time to develop, mentor and support new project managers running their first projects can actually yield a substantial benefit to future successes during in-house project delivery.

So how can your organisation get better at developing and mentoring great internal PMs?

Be very strict on the fundamentals

The core fundamentals of project management are critical for a new project manager to get right, starting at a project's inception and sustained throughout the duration of the project.

Being disciplined with core fundamentals has a twofold effect: it instils good habits that hold a project manager in good stead for the future and, more importantly, serve to build confidence within the wider stakeholder group that the project is well managed.

For example, project deliverables that should be followed to the letter include:

- Crisp, on-time reporting across all project KPI's (scope, financials, risks etc.)
- Detailed schedules that are regularly updated

- Key project meetings held regularly
- Timely production of minutes
- Strict change control processes for scope changes

Experienced project managers can and do look to cut corners with project fundamentals depending on the environment and the project challenges they face.

Not every project is a paint-by-numbers exercise and with a risk-based assessment approach, experienced project managers can find time and cost savings during delivery.

A typical example may be discontinuing a project forum that is not adding value or scaling back certain reporting requirements for example.

Picking and choosing which project fundamentals can be scaled back is not a luxury an inexperienced project manager can enjoy. They should – at all times – be adhering to the key project fundamentals and executing them diligently.

You can delay but not avoid the fiery furnace

Interestingly the most recent update to PMBOK (5th edition) has finally included Stakeholder Management as a stand-alone core competency of project management.

It could be argued that stakeholder management is at the heart of good project management – get it wrong and all the fundamentals in the world will not save the project manager.

We believe the elevation of Stakeholder Management to a core competency of PMBOK is long overdue and recognises successfully managing projects is not just about following process but also managing people, some difficult and often much more senior than the project manager.

Whilst the PMBOK guide and other relevant project literature can help prepare a new project manager to become a successful stakeholder manager, it cannot replace real life experience. To gain experience in stakeholder management the best way is to be thrown into difficult and challenging situations.

New project managers should be encouraged to attend not avoid difficult stakeholder forums, meet the challenges of dissatisfied stakeholders head on and take some knocks along the way. It is this scar tissue that built up over time (known as 'experience'!) that is essential to the development of a project manager.

Keeping a new project manager out of the firing line may make tactical sense for the current project but it will hinder rather than help their longer-term development.

Give them some of the 'A' team

Projects cannot be delivered successfully without good people on the team. A new project manager may not have the experience to discern who on their team is pulling hard in their direction or is perhaps disengaged or lacking core skills.

It is therefore critical to make sure new project managers have good, experienced people within some of the key project roles to support them.

This may be a challenge for the PMO, as typically inexperienced project managers are not given the high profile or risky projects and thus miss out on having access to the best delivery personnel.

But if the aim is to nurture and develop a new project manager then thought must be given to surrounding them with a few excellent operators, who will not only help show what good delivery is but can also be used in a mentoring capacity as well.

A longer-term view of project management capability

The pay-off of to future successful project delivery can be substantial to an organisation if they can mentor and develop project capability in house. Like any competency project managers need time and support to develop their skills when entering the profession.

Whilst not exhaustive hopefully the above list provides a few practical pointers to organisations when considering how best to mentor and develop new project managers internally.

Building the right project team: A critical enabler for success.

How can you consistently replicate the successes of effective project delivery? The answer lies in the teams you build.

No matter what the endeavour, selecting and engaging the right team is a critical enabler for success. This holds particularly true for organisations that may have to build (and subsequently disband) multiple project teams in any given year.

Highly functional project teams do not happen by accident. At their core is a sound selection and engagement process that occurs at the formation stage of the team.

Like most things, it's not an exact science, but there are certainly some guidelines that will increase the chances of getting the team mix right.

Define – then target – the right skills

The first critical activity in building a project team is to drive out the roles and responsibilities for each team member, then document the skill set required for each role.

While it sounds simple enough, this provides clarity of the base capability required for the team to be successful.

Unfortunately, it's an all-too-often occurrence that teams are pulled together with both a misunderstanding of what the roles are and also whether the people within the team have the right skills for their respective responsibilities.

For example, a common team-building mistake is appointing Subject Matter Experts into the role of Business Analysts. These are different roles with different skill sets. Time should always be set aside to understand fully what skills are needed for each role (the minimum base skills and the "nice to haves").

During the on-boarding process interviews should be conducted – even for internal resources – to thoroughly drill into the potential team members expertise to ensure the person has the required skills base before they are engaged.

Culture is critical

The right skills is only part of the equation however. The next critical piece is culture. A key question is whether the person will fit into the team and work well with others in the team, customers, suppliers and stakeholders.

This is a difficult thing to ascertain and it does require some gut instinct once you've gone through the usual process of interviews, reference checks and other due diligence.

We feel that it is much better to get the right cultural fit with a skills gap than the other way around. A skills gap can be detrimental to the team but can usually be contained and addressed in a systematic way, such as training.

A team member with a poor attitude, on the other hand, can significantly undermine a project from within and be almost impossible to remedy. Attitudes, especially poor ones, are very difficult to change.

So our guidance is to pay special attention to the cultural fit of all team members as it could be the difference between a harmonious, high functioning team or a soul-sapping forced march for all involved.

Should you look inside or outside?

Looking for team members from within or outside your organisation depends on a number of factors.

In a perfect world, it should be the best person for the job regardless of whether they are internal or external, however often hiring policies and/or budget constraints dictate where the resources come from. Usually the first option is to look internal.

The challenge with internal resources is that they may not have the right skill set or, if they do, there may be bandwidth issues. Also projects are sometimes so contentious that it's preferable to bring in external resources, particularly for the more senior roles.

Either way, when establishing a new team, consideration should be given to looking both inside and outside the organisation where permitted and using the same hiring criteria for each person irrespective of the source.

When stuck, work with what you've got

There's a famous scene from a Clint Eastwood film where a recently promoted soldier celebrates his newly bestowed ranking as his just reward, to which his superior says: "You're not the best man for the job, just the best one that is still alive."

It can be the same with project teams (even if they are not life and death). The right person for the job may not be available to the team because of commitments to another role, budget constraints that don't allow for the right money to attract the right person or because of internal/external hiring restrictions.

If you cannot get the exact fit, compromises will need to be made to retain project momentum.

If this does occur engaging a person with gaps in their required skill set should also be accompanied with plans to augment the gaps, such as targeted mentoring, mixing and matching deliverables with other team members who do have the right skill set or providing suitable training.

Be prepared for some flex and refinement

The guidelines above are helpful for establishing a successful project team from scratch, however even if you follow them all to the letter, it's still not a guarantee for success.

The way teams form and then work together, particularly when placed under pressure, will not really be known until the time comes.

While there are no guarantees, following some of the basics like the above will give your teams far better opportunity for success than failure when attempting to establish skilled, harmonious and high-functioning teams.

CHAPTER 4
DEVELOPING BETTER PROJECT SPONSORS

Managing success with a first time sponsor

How can project management fundamentals support a first-time sponsor to deliver a program effectively?

The success or otherwise of a project often comes down to the quality of the team that can be assembled.

For critical roles like the project manager prudent organisations will invest significant time and resource in the selection process. Whilst there is little barrier to entry for many roles within a project team this selection process can ensure a certain quality of capability across the board when a project team is being pulled together.

Paradoxically whilst significant care is taken in selecting a team to run a project the one role that often escapes any serious scrutiny is that of the sponsor, arguably the most important role of all within the project structure.

So what are the challenges a project manager will face if they have a new or inexperienced first time sponsor and what can be done to bridge this gap to ensure project success?

It is 'our' project not 'my' project

The first thing a project manager needs to convey to a new sponsor is their accountability of ownership of the outcomes. It should be made clear the project manager is not owning the project but is delivering the project on behalf of the sponsor and they will need to work effectively together to be successful.

From the earliest discussions the project manager should start to build this collaborative relationship. Emphasising the project is a joint endeavour and the success or otherwise of the project will depend on how well they both work together as a team.

Step the sponsor through the roles and responsibilities ... then repeat

The roles and responsibilities is an often-neglected document. It is furnished at the initial kick-off meetings then shelved as the project sets off on a course of all hands on deck to meet deliverables. Nonetheless clarity on roles and responsibilities within projects should be front and centre when engaging a new sponsor.

Not only does this set out what is required of project sponsor but will also provide excellent context for the sponsor as to what everybody else is doing. It should be referred to as often as required and be used as a tool to continually reinforce what is expected of the sponsor in their role.

Enable the sponsor to be successful by creating the right forums

It can be lonely at the top and confusing as well, especially for a first time sponsor. The project manager should be ensuring the sponsor has the right support from the right people to help them execute their role successfully.

To do this the project manager should ensure the key forums, like the steering committee, are established early on in the life of a project, the attendees are the right people and everybody is walked through and sign up to the roles and responsibilities.

These meetings must then be run regularly and effectively. They are critical forums in assisting all sponsors - especially an inexperienced one - to make the best possible decisions for the good of the project.

Be flexible with the demands on your sponsor's time

Alas project managers will never have the luxury of a sponsor being 100% dedicated for the life of a project. They have day jobs, often extremely demanding ones at that, and a myriad of non project related issues to deal with on a regular basis. The project manager must be cognisant of these other competing demands.

They need to make it as easy as possible for the sponsor to meet their project responsibilities. They should be empathetic to a sponsor's competing priorities and flexible as required. This is especially true for a new sponsor.

The project manager should quickly come to grips with the sponsor's monthly timetable, where are their busy points and identify the best opportunities to get clear access and structure the project meetings and forums accordingly.

Collaboration and relationship building is vital

A successful project is always the result of sound collaboration and the most important relationship is between the sponsor and the project manager. It is inevitable that from time to time a new sponsor will be appointed to a project and the building of this collaborative relationship will need extra care and attention.

Whilst the above list is not exhaustive it provides some key actions a project manager can consider when faced with a new and inexperienced first time sponsor.

Developing better project sponsors

One of the foundation stones of successful project delivery is, without question, solid sponsorship. However, the definition of what makes a 'good' sponsor is often misunderstood.

Sponsors are typically appointed as a result of rising through the ranks and reaching C level status.

Having a solid grounding in business-as-usual (BAU) doesn't necessarily prepare them adequately for sponsoring projects.

So how can you ensure new or existing sponsors understand the demands of sponsorship and help them to be better sponsors?

Ownership – It's your project not theirs

A fundamental part of being a successful sponsor is the acknowledgement that you own the benefits and ultimate outcomes of the project. Your team may execute the project on your behalf, but they do not own the project – you do.

As the sponsor, your role is to foster strong collaboration between you and the project team to help drive the project to being a success, but ultimately the ownership of the delivering the successful outcomes lies with you.

Context – Where does your project fit into the program?

It is critical that a sponsor knows and understands where their project or stream fits into the overall change strategy of the organisation. Rarely are projects delivered in a vacuum and the knowledge of where your particular projects fits is critical to be an effective sponsor.

This strategic context enables the sponsor to better explain to the team why certain things are important and get their buy in. The team will inherently have an expectation the sponsor is across the wider change agenda anyway and expect the sponsor to be able to articulate the change vision.

Also the understanding of the myriad of potential interdependencies greatly assists a sponsor when assessing priorities and helping with critical decisions.

Management – Engage the team

More often than not sponsors will have day jobs that run alongside their sponsorship role, which may limit the opportunity to interact with the project.

Line management responsibilities often do not allow sponsors to spend extended periods of time with a project team or even get to know the team members below the immediate leadership, for example, the project manager, change manager etc.

Teams function much better when they are positive engaged by the leadership. As a sponsor, ensure you take the time to:

- Meet and get to know the team members
- Understand who is who
- Be visible and available as much as possible especially during key milestones.
- Lead the celebration of successes and participate in post mortem when the team comes up short.

Your project manager should help guide you with the 'who's who' and the timings of when you need to be visible and actively engaged with the team. In short be prepared to treat the team as part of your overall team for the duration of the project.

Leadership – Make decisions

Few things are more damaging to a project's momentum and team harmony than the inability to make decisions. It can be argued that a sub-optimal decision trumps a non-decision every time.

Projects drive change and change by its nature requires decisions and sometimes they will not always be easy decisions to make.

A good sponsor will be aware of this and ensure during project establishment the correct governance forums and decision-making frameworks are put in place.

They will also ensure they actively participate in the decision-making process as required and the decisions are considered and well thought through and made in a timely manner.

Confidence – Be bold in your decision-making

Change that adds true value to an organisation often requires the making of difficult decisions. This holds true for many projects. Good sponsors do not shy away from the contentious decisions if they are the right ones.

Be bold. Trust your instincts, those of your team and look to maximise the outcomes for the projects by going for the decision profile that will maximise the benefits.

Context – Live the roles and responsibilities

Roles and responsibilities are not only the guidelines of how you – as a sponsor – need to conduct yourself during the project they also provide the context of how the rest of the project team see your role.

It's important for team discipline and morale that you work within the guidelines of the roles and responsibilities, execute yours to the best of your ability and also understand and respect the project team members' roles and responsibilities.

Be willing to see the nuances

Sponsoring projects is not a paint by numbers exercise. All projects will have their nuances and different personalities and challenges.

Sponsoring projects is not an exact science but there are some fundamentals that hold true for all projects. Whilst the above list is not exhaustive it is a good reference guide if you want to be the best sponsor you can be.

The Good Sponsor Guide: Setting Up IT Projects for Success

How can bringing business sponsors and IT expertise together ensure that change initiatives are set up for success?

The fast-paced nature of business change means that more and more business change initiatives have a significant IT component. More often than not, business people sponsor the change initiatives, not the IT projects related to them.

Ultimately, projects are set up to deliver a specific outcome and the sponsor is accountable for realising those outcomes across all streams of the project. This accountability includes IT deliverables within the project.

So what are the challenges that a business sponsor needs to consider when their projects have an IT component and how should they select the best team to set the project up for success?

Best Practice: Who is the right sponsor?

Best practice suggests that the sponsor for most projects is the person who owns the most benefits the project is designed to deliver. Where that is not clear cut, then the alternative would be to consider the person whose organisation is most impacted by the change.

Project sponsors are typically supported by other key representatives in the business – normally a steering committee – whose organisations are either impacted by the change or who will actively contribute to the changes.

In many instances, a senior IT representative will have a seat at the table, assisting the business sponsor with the project's technical scope and challenges.

The importance of a single Project Manager

The role of the Project Manager in delivering business projects is a vital one, so selecting the right person and defining the scope of their role is critical for the sponsor.

As project specialists, Quay subscribes to the philosophy that there should only be one project manager on any given project and their role is to plan, monitor and control the delivery of the full scope of the project on behalf of the sponsor.

This means active management of both the business change and the IT contribution required to enable the change. The various streams, including IT, can and should have leads where appropriate but the final responsibility to deliver the overall outcomes should rest with a single project manager.

Bring IT into the tent

IT, by its nature, is full of specialists and specialists have their way of doing things that may or may not be in the best interest of the project's business objectives. It's important that the business sponsor sets up the project organisation structure to ensure that IT is in the tent.

The IT lead must report into the Project Manager as a team member irrespective of whether they are internal or a vendor. There can be a lack of context around the ultimate outcome of IT's deliverables if they are left outside the main project team, because the best "IT solution" is not always the best business solution.

It's an area that requires active debate and agreement and the business sponsor needs to ensure that IT is an active part of the project structure to minimise risk.

Collaboration between IT and the business

As the IT landscape morphs more and more into a "Service" based environment, IT will need to focus on integrating services to provide business process rather than developing bespoke software applications.

This shift, and a general demand for faster delivery, has led to widespread adoption of agile project delivery. We all interpret the written word differently based upon our experiences – agile delivery allows discussion, visualisation, collaboration and rapid delivery to ensure what is needed matches what is delivered.

This means the business sponsor must put their best people together with the IT specialists to make the magic happen.

Don't forget if they have a day job these competing demands need to be actively managed.

Projects impact IT and end users alike

The business sponsor must remain cognisant of the fact that in addition to the business impact the project will deliver, there are also organisational and customer impacts.

As the project will impact IT, the sponsor must make allowance for the operational impact on IT to support the solution. In some cases, this may translate to additional IT head count and operational cost, which must be factored into the business case from the beginning to reflect the true total cost of ownership.

Ensure IT endorse the solution

Finally, it's important that the business sponsor secures the endorsement of their organisation's IT rule book to ensure the IT components of the project are complimentary to the existing IT ecosystem.

This ensures that the business doesn't unintentionally introduce new technology that is unsupported by IT and that a senior IT representative has endorsed any expenditure for the chosen solution. This doesn't mean that the business shouldn't introduce new technology but rather that collaboration between business and its IT team will likely yield a far better outcome for integration, adoption and support.

Due to the fast pace of business change Projects will increasingly have critical and more complex IT components that need to be managed.

Whilst it is not expected that business sponsors need to be IT specialists the above list, whilst not exhaustive, offers a good guide to some of the steps a business sponsor can take to ensure they achieve successful IT outcomes for their projects, no matter the complexity.

CHAPTER 5
HOW TO TRANSFORM

The value of a Transformation Office in achieving stakeholder alignment

Undertaking transformation is challenging for any organisation, however achieving alignment between stakeholders is vital to its success.

Successful transformation in any organisation relies on the alignment of stakeholders across the business, from board level right through to the front line. Transformation usually affects everyone within an organisation and while existing PMOs are vital for the delivery of programs and projects, a Transformation Office enables the organisation to establish a mandate for transformation and the ability to determine the highest priorities when it comes to implementing and effecting change.

So what is a transformation office and how does it differ from a project management office (PMO)

What is a Transformation Office?

A Transformation Office is typically a temporary governance and delivery vehicle whose sole purpose is to govern and drive the successful implementation of critical programs or projects that enable the organisation be transformed.

However the role of the Transformation Office extends beyond governance and reporting on the programs and projects being undertaken.

A Transformation Office should also lead the implementation of the Transformation Program's functions and activities, securing investment for its establishment and oversee its evolution to contribute to achievement of the organisational objectives.

As transformation touches everyone in the organisation, consideration should be given to having the report to a Transformation Board comprised of the C-Suite executives who will be faced with making key decisions to support the change being undertaken.

A strong Transformation Board is a critical success factor in achieving the transformation goals and dealing head on with conflicting priorities that face the different aspects of the organisation.

The C-Suite working together ensures the breadth of alignment required to make things happen.

The Transformation Office needs to balance competing demands across the programs and work closely with the Transformation Board to prioritise and manage inevitable conflicts such as limited subject matter expert resources and project versus business as usual constraints.

Furthermore, the Transformation Office needs to ensure that the projects within its scope are delivered against agreed business criteria, and embed good project management disciplines across the program.

Aligning project delivery to transformation goals

The key functions therefore for a Transformation Office can:

- Provide leadership for the implementation of the Transformation Program, coordinating and directing activities to achieve the overall objectives of the organisation
- Secure the investment to implement the Program and maximise the return on investment for the organisation
- Develop the Portfolio Strategy and Delivery Plan (for Opex and Capex related projects) to align with the overall strategy and plan of the organisation
- Ensure the portfolio evolves as needed to reflect changes in overall strategic objectives and business priorities
- Oversee the allocation of resources to ensure resourcing reflects demand and need
- Oversee portfolio management practice documentation and the preparation of investment data to ensure records and information are accurate and up-to-date
- Prioritise the investment portfolio for approval by the TB

- Drive the Transformation agenda and value capture initiatives within the Transformation Office to consistently deliver efficiency and set a platform for increased commerciality
- Motivate, encourage and inspire the development of a strong, efficient and effective professional team operating ethically and with a clear focus on delivering outcomes

So how does a Transformation Office work with an existing PMO?

What sets a Transformation Office apart from most PMOs is that it has the mandate to transform the organisation and governance from within the C-Suite, which ensures it has the highest priority when coming to implementing and effecting change.

In most aspects a Transformation Office is aligned to a Program Delivery PMO in that it is a temporary endeavour that survives for the duration of the program. Once the transformation is complete the Transformation Office is normally disbanded.

Where an Enterprise PMO exists, the Transformation Office needs to work with the ePMO in order to ensure application of fit for purpose delivery approach and controls.

It can be the case that where differences in approach between the ePMO and the Transformation Office exist the Transformation Office shall prevail due to the special and temporary nature of its objectives as opposed to the steadier state role often played by an ePMO.

Resourcing a Transformation Office

Considered thought should therefore be taken when looking at resourcing the Transformation Office to understand what happens to those resources post transformation.

In some instances, it may be better to hire in the skills required for the duration so as to avoid competition for limited post Transformation Office permanent roles in the organisation.

Delivering transformation success

Undertaking transformation is challenging for any organisation, however achieving alignment between stakeholders is vital to its success.

One of the key reasons that a Transformation Office can ensure successful transformation delivery is that its objectives are to drive alignment and ensure that the objectives of transformation are met, rather than being distracted by the objectives of specific programs of work.

Balancing transformation demands with a day job

Most organisations that Quay works with are going through some form of transformation and whilst approaches to transformation differ, what is consistent is that in all cases the Subject Matter Experts (SMEs) are heavily involved in the process.

Which leads us to the question: How can they balance the demands of a transformation role without compromising the responsibilities of their day job?

The challenge of a 'matrixed approach'

We call this balancing act a 'matrixed approach' to project delivery, where the business-as-usual (BAU) reporting lines and functions remain unchanged, however a new reporting line and function is added for SME participation in the transformation project.

In summary, they now have two jobs, two bosses, more work and often conflicting priorities. Our experience – and that of Quay's clients – is that these SMEs tend to work longer and harder to ensure their day jobs continue unimpeded, whilst also enabling them to provide input into the transformation. While this increased level of effort is commendable, it is also unsustainable. There is a tangible risk that these SMEs will get burned out and/or that quality will suffer.

Helping SMEs to get the balance right

The reality of SME involvement in transformation projects is that the BAU work still needs to get done. In many cases, there will not be sufficient funding to provide resource backfill and as such, SMEs need to manage both their day and project jobs.

Management needs to acknowledge the dual roles SMEs play and enable them to manage both sets of responsibilities by facilitating different ways of working. For example:

- Looking at where duplication and/or unnecessary effort can be eliminated
- Challenging the necessity of some tasks

Moving to exception-based task management to free up project time without impacting what the business needs and the quality of what's provided.

The cost of not actively managing change

Actively challenging BAU past practices, looking at process improvement and supporting staff to work in a different way is as essential as managing the change process within transformation itself.

Without the support of management, staff will naturally work longer hours rather than change the way they function to get the work done.

This of course can lead to burnout and sub-optimal performance, or in the worst case scenario, departure from the business. These negative impacts have a direct bottom line impact to the business.

The cost of burnout and reduced performance affects business as usual work, but the real detriment is delivered to the cost and quality of the transformation itself – a real double whammy.

Ensuring On-Going success for Transformation Programs

Transformation programs tend to run for years rather than months. How can you ensure the program is set up for continuous success for the duration?

A key characteristic of transformation programs that sets them apart from most other large scale projects is that they tend to run for years rather than months, requiring a sustained effort and focus over a long period of time.

Guarding against fatigue for the people delivering a transformation program is essential, however what else needs to be considered to ensure the program is set up for continuous success throughout its life cycle?

There are a number of key challenges that should be taken into consideration when executing a multi-year transformation.

Do not set and forget

The streams within a transformation program can change over time as scope is delivered and the nature of future initiatives can be quite different from previously agreed deliverables.

For example, the initial phases of a transformation could be to implement an Enterprise Resource Plan (ERP) with a large emphasis on IT activities. Subsequent phases may then focus on Business Process Re-engineering to unlock the value of the system, which requires greater business input and leadership.

The transformation executives overseeing the program need to be cognizant of the changing nature of the streams and ensure the governance structures (including the key stakeholders who participate) are appropriate. They should also be mindful that the various control authorities and processes are regularly reviewed and adjusted as required so they remain fit for purpose.

Consider refreshing your sponsor

This is important for two reasons. Firstly, as the transformation program progresses the focus on the outcomes could shift from one business unit to another.

So the original sponsor at the establishment of the program may no longer be the most appropriate or logical sponsor one or two years down the track.

Secondly, the skill set required to energise all key stakeholders behind the initiatives and to get a program up and running, can differ from the skill set required for the longer haul of sustained execution.

Always make it bite sized

Transformations by their very nature are large, complex initiatives.

Regardless of size, the key project delivery fundamental of breaking down initiatives into smaller components that are more easily managed should not be ignored.

In fact avoiding the big bang approach becomes even more important. So effort should be put in during the planning phases of the program to deliver in discreet, manageable releases.

Communicate early and often

Getting the organisation energised around a transformation program requires a significant amount of up front communication and user engagement.

Once the business is engaged it is important to keep them so. Ensure the focus is maintained on the communications and change activities during the life of the program.

Those inside the program who are living and breathing it will remain engaged but the outside world may quickly move on and forget if not regularly reminded of why the program is underway and its importance.

Transformation programs are not just for Christmas

Often the initial establishment and engagement of the business can be the easy part of a transformation program.

Executing a successful transformation that leaves the business in better shape requires sustained effort and regular calibration to make sure the governance, processes, people and messaging is always fit for purpose for whatever phase the transformation is in.

Managing project fatigue during transition programs

Successful project delivery requires highly functioning teams with a common purpose – so how do you manage project fatigue?

A key factor in successful project delivery is developing and maintaining highly functional teams who share a single common purpose.

But what if the program is a lengthy transformation with multiple milestones and the final outcome of the program is not always easy to define and communicate?

Managing the risk of project fatigue

The best project managers are expert in building clarity of purpose and shared commitment within their teams, and have the ability to harness both to achieve successful delivery during a single-sustained push to the summit.

Developing a shared, common purpose and keeping a team motivated (and on task) becomes increasingly problematic during lengthy transformations.

Project fatigue is a constant risk and the sponsor and transformation executive should be alert to the detrimental impacts to the outcomes when it starts to set in.

There are a number of steps that can be taken to limit the impact of project fatigue during a transformation program both within the project teams and the wider business.

Keep reminding everybody why we are here again

This is the flag on the hill that is driving the entire transformation program. Be prepared to regularly engage the senior executive to communicate to the team and wider audience why the transformation and their role within it remains important to the organisation.

Invest the time up front in portfolio planning

Whilst a transformation is by its nature a journey of discovery over an extended period, the ability to provide a sequenced road map even at the high level, can be a very powerful tool to keep project teams engaged.

The way to do this is investing the time up front in the portfolio pre-planning stage so the project teams have a understanding of how their piece fits into the bigger picture and the longer term objectives.

Refresh the team with new blood

Not everybody is predisposed to the long haul of constant project execution so be prepared to regularly refresh and mix up teams with new blood.

This could mean bringing in externals for defined pieces of work, mixing up project teams once projects are complete or swapping business people in and out of teams so they remain refreshed and motivated.

Regularly assess if the benefits remain valid

Not unlike reminding the team why we are all still here, it is imperative as the program extends into the outer reaches of the transformation road map to have regular checkpoints to ensure the business environment has not changed to the point that the project is not worth doing. Nothing de-motivates a team more if they cannot see or do not understand the benefits of the project they are working on.

Be prepared to reset the program regularly

A reset can take many forms and is a very effective way to keep project teams on message and motivated. It can be via regular communication or forums and often goes hand in hand with implementing learnings from the project's assurance function.

Project teams are very aware of process disconnects so be prepared to keep refreshing the approach where applicable.

Celebrate success

Typically, the reward for successful project delivery is to give the team another project. Move beyond this and work with the project manager to identify a meaningful rewards program that acknowledges the team's efforts and suitably compensates and motivates them to keep delivering.

A certain amount of project fatigue during a lengthy transformation is inevitable but by awareness of the risks and following some of the above mitigations will help ensure you keep getting the best out of the project teams and they remain engaged and motivated.

Delivering Technology Transformation

Improving efficiency, scalability and cost reduction are key drivers for technology transformation, however it is vital that IT aligns with the business to deliver change successfully.

Changing market forces can make a compelling case for technology transformation in many organisations, demanding greater efficiency, scalability, cost reduction and integration across departments.

It's not uncommon to find as an organisation grows there is a risk of duplication in roles, processes and technology, particularly where growth has been achieved through acquisition or strong business units that see their key strength as being independent from the 'mothership.'

Although the opportunity to improve service, reduce cost and increase efficiency can be significant and on face value a compelling reason to transform, many businesses are often challenged to make the right business decisions due to agenda's driven from silos or the complexity of the challenge.

So what prevents organisations taking steps to transform and what is the best approach to gaining approval and then delivering successful technology transformation?

Mistrust of IT and its ability to deliver.

One major blocker is the inherent mistrust the business has in IT's capability to deliver major transformations.

In many instances, IT is seen as a support to the business rather than as a strategic enabler. As such delays, overruns and failures can prove fatal to the technology transformation business case.

Where successful, IT has been able to position themselves as an enabler and someone that works alongside the business as a strategic partner and helps influence the right decisions rather than just being seen as an execution arm.

Lack of alignment

Not being able to align with the business is a significant blocker for transformation. A sure-fire way to halt any initiative in its tracks is failing the WIFM test i.e. "What's in it for me?".

This typically occurs when IT fails to sell or show clearly what the benefits are for the business.

In the case of successful transformation projects, these have typically had senior IT leadership work hard with the heads of the business to get their engagement, a process that focuses on building:

- Relationships
- Trust
- Evidence of delivery capability
- Demonstration of delivery capacity
- Value to the business
- Cost effectiveness
- Knowledge and acceptance of impact (No pain no gain)

Compelling event – Strong Business Case

There is nothing quite like a burning platform to drive through transformations that results in increased efficiency, reduced operating costs or increased revenue.

Creating or identifying that compelling event and articulating it in a way that the business can understand can help ensure you gain approval and on-going support for the life of the transformation.

Let's assume that IT has been able to align with the business and become a strategic enabler, have created the compelling event and have a signed-off business case. Congratulations – that's no small feat. The next challenge is to successfully deliver the technology transformation.

Setting Transformations up for success

Some of the key ingredients required to ensure a technology transformation is successful include:

Passion and conviction from the top

Strong and unified sponsorship from the executive is a critical success enabler. Few – if any – organisations find change easy. A strong and passionate focus on the benefits of the transformation from the top down helps to ensure buy-in across the organisation.

Anticipating and mitigating risks that may derail the program and maintaining high levels of energy and momentum is key especially when the delivery requires hard graft.

Strong alignment with business owners and change champions

Building trust at all levels of management and leadership is critical for success. Working with the business from the first hypothetical discussions to delivering a fully operational IT transformation is essential. Building trust by collaborative working on each element of the program means you can have robust discussions when required to ensure constant achievement of quality.

Use a fit for purpose PM framework

Each organisation has its own delivery DNA which brings the ingredients for success. A right-sized governance framework, with appropriate levels of reporting and documentation across a consistent format will help ensure success. Combining this with a "no surprises" policy ensures that issues are identified early, tracked consistently and informed decisions can be made.

People are key

Capability and culture are two key ingredients for the right team. Cultural alignment above all else can jeopardise success. Hand picking the right people or partners with the rights skills and right values, behaviours and attitude is critical. Constantly monitoring and injecting new energy and capability can be a good tactic if momentum is wavering.

Winning breeds winners

Short, sharp, regular and achievable goals are great for building a winning feel in the process that is technology transformation – or indeed any broad change within an organisation.

Keeping scope achievable and being brave enough to scale back if required helps maintain this momentum. With trust and buy in from the business this is easier to achieve.

It's not about technology

IT is a business enabler. Transformation is to support business objectives. Unless the business processes and capabilities in the business are also improved IT can never be successful.

Transformation should include two separate streams, IT and business change. Decoupling dependencies between change and IT can ensure one does not delay the other.

Change and transformation is never easy.

There are a number of measures and approaches we have explored above to gain buy in and maintain momentum to achieve successful technology transformation. Whilst the technology remains very important it cannot be addressed in isolation. The people, relationships and trust remain critical for the success of any transformation.

CHAPTER 6
PMOS: THE HOWS AND THE WHYS

Converting program PMOs into enterprise PMOs

Standalone PMOs enable organisations to run large programs of work efficiently.

PMOs create and manage the controls and standards around project delivery, assist with portfolio management and provide a single point for reporting requirements.

Typically, when a program concludes, there is no need for the program PMO to continue. However there still remains a need for an Enterprise PMO (EPMO) to manage steady state projects.

These projects are:

- Often focused on compliance and BAU
- Do not have the same risk, cost and complexity profile of large transformational programs; and
- Require a different set of PMO resources and controls.

Organisations that have completed a large-scale program of work either do not have an equivalent EPMO or if they did, it has often been downgraded in terms of resources, structures and importance due to the large program that has been in train.

In these circumstances the organisation has an opportunity to leverage the structure of the program PMO to take forward as the organisation's EPMO.

How is a program PMO different to an EPMO?

A program PMO is different to an EPMO in a number of subtle yet important ways. It's important for an organisation to understand these differences and take steps to modify the structure and charter of the outgoing program PMO if it is morph successfully into a EPMO for the organisation.

We have listed below a number of differences that should be taken into consideration during this process.

Understand scale

An organisation just completing a large transformational program may have a reduced slate of future project activity with less risk and complexity. In this instance the new EPMO should be scaled accordingly, with potentially lighter project controls, resourcing and reporting requirements to ensure it is fit for purpose.

Annual master planning exercise

Typically, a large program has its high level scope and cost understood and quarantined up front. With an EPMO there may be a requirement to have a regular master planning exercise to identify and agree the type and sequencing of the annual project activity.

The EPMO should be modified to ensure it has the ability to help facilitate a regular master planning exercise mapping back to strategy as well as meet any portfolio management requirements.

Is the governance fit-for-purpose?

Typically, the program PMO would be underpinning by a complex governance structure and a well-defined business engagement model.

The new EPMO may need to have some additional controls in place if the new governance is lighter on due to the less critical nature of the slate of projects.

New business stakeholders will need to be identified and the relationships understood and included as part of a revised business engagement model.

Is assurance still fit-for-purpose?

Often with large programs the project assurance is heavily skewed towards gate reviews and lengthy and costly point in time health checks.

With smaller, less critical compliance and BAU projects this type of assurance may no longer be fit-for-purpose. Steps should be taken to ensure the external assurance meets the new requirements.

This could mean less large, formal reviews and shorter, reviews like start up reviews and targeted PIRs.

The above list is not meant to be exhaustive but an indicator of a few of the key areas organisations need to consider if they intend to embark on leveraging a program PMO into a EPMO.

Creating a transformational PMO

How can PMOs utilise existing services and capabilities to ensure the right transformation levers are in place?

There are enormous benefits for an organisation to have a PMO that is both well run and provides a fit-for-purpose set of services and capabilities to meet the organisation's project requirements.

However, an Enterprise PMO (EPMO) that is supporting a business-as-usual slate of projects may not have the levers required to help an organisation deliver a transformational program of work.

Organisations embarking on a large transformational program of work need to undertake a gap analysis to ensure the EPMO is set up to function as a Transformation Office to support the transformation.

Defining the organisational structure for EPMO

Consideration should also be given as to where the EPMO sits in the organisation during the transformation.

EMPOs can sit under Finance where cost savings are driving the portfolio of projects or under IT where large scale IT upgrades and infrastructure projects dominate the program of works.

However, where the business is truly transforming it works best sitting under a Transformational Governance Board that ensures alignment of CFO, COO, CIO and CEO – each of whom have different drivers. To achieve transformation goals this group needs to be aligned and make enterprise decisions brought to them by the EPMO.

While it is not an exact science and each organisation will have different areas of emphasis, there are potential service areas that EPMOs should be providing or have significant involvement in to make sure that a transformation program is properly constructed and managed.

Provide a Portfolio View

Transformation programs typically attract much greater interest at the executive level where access to a portfolio view of interrelated programs and projects is required.

The EPMO needs to create consistency and visibility of reporting including inter-dependencies, dependencies, constraints and resource allocation across the portfolio as well as identification of key risks and issues facing the Transformation Program. Utilising a Master Scheduler can be a powerful way to achieve this.

Furthermore, there is solid logic that the EPMO also manages the view of the Organisations Resources as well. Managing change is complex and often the same resources are needed for competing projects.

By having centralised visibility of the capacity of the organisation, the Transformation Governance Board can make informed decisions and prioritise which project(s) get which resources and when or if they need to be externally funded and sourced resources to address gaps.

Create stage gates for an Enterprise Design Authority

Before any approvals are given to solutions that deliver components of the Transformation Program, there should be an early stage gate whereby an Enterprise Design Authority (or similar body) ensures the solutions are compatible with the long-arm architecture of the organisation.

This will help guard against execution of projects that work at cross purposes with each other or are difficult to integrate and support within an organisation's IT architecture.

The EPMO should help manage and control this gating process to ensure it is set up, is well understood by all participants and outcomes regularly tracked and reported against.

Focus on the Business Case template and processes

With transformational programs there is often significant blue sky in the estimation of the benefits.

An organisation is typically executing new types of projects and for that reason they are harder to estimate the exact costs and benefits as accurately as a BAU project that has been delivered in the past.

Furthermore, there is increased competition from projects all wanting access to the same funding from the transformational funding pot.

It is important that during a transformation program the Business Case template and processes are well thought out, easy to use and have the ability to generate diagnostics that allow decision makers to confidently select the right projects to include in the overall program.

Utilise existing PMO services, capabilities and levers

The list above is not an exhaustive one and all organisations have their own delivery DNA – the things they do well, or not so well, and different areas of focus.

Moving your EPMO to support a transformation program requires that you take stock of the services and capabilities currently provided by the PMO to ensure the right levers are in place for the transformation program's success.

EPMO – Friend or Foe?

Statistics suggested that the typical lifespan of a PMO is eighteen months, a sobering statistic by anyone's standards when considering the dollars at stake in delivering successful projects and change.

Given that the role of an Enterprise Program Management Office (EPMO) is to strategically align an organisation's goals and provide multiple program management offices (PMOs), why is it that so many PMOs and EPMOs fail to deliver and what is the value add that a strategically aligned EPMO can provide?

The purpose of an EPMO

The role of an EPMO is multifaceted: its capability exists to collect, analyse and display program data in a way that enables executives to see at a glance how well their programs are running and consequently how overall project delivery is progressing.

In short, an EPMO can be a powerful strategic partner to the executive by providing vital information on business critical programs.

Why do PMOs and EPMOs fail?

The barrier to successfully setting up and running an effective EPMO are largely driven by two things:

- Is the organisation ready for it (maturity)?
- Does the EPMO provide value?

When the answer to these to questions is yes then an EPMO can grow and flourish, providing value to the organisation. If the answer to either question is no, then the challenge is to demonstrate the value of what an EPMO can deliver.

As mentioned above, the average lifespan of a PMO is approximately eighteen months. Research has identified seven core reasons for this:

- The PMO did not define its value proposition.

- The PMO is not perceived as impacting project delivery capabilities.
- The PMO is seen as a threat (often because it is too authoritative).
- The PMO is too low in the management reporting structure.
- The PMO does not have buy-in from senior functional managers.
- The PMO is seen as micro managing and attempting to directly control every project.
- The PMO acronym becomes Project Management Overhead.

Considering the causes above for failure, how can EPMOs succeed and deliver value to an organisation?

Setting up a sustainable EPMO

There are four key drivers for success in setting up an EPMO:

- Pitch the EPMO at the level the Organisation is ready for not what you think it needs.
- Ensure you align the EPMO with the organisations business needs
- Bring energy, knowledge and persistence to setting up an EPMO. It is a marathon not a sprint.
- Executive sponsorship is key. Prepare to education and win over the key sponsors to ensure success.

If you can achieve the above, the value a strategically savvy EPMO can provide includes:

- Visibility and clarity to the organisation and its management teams
- Acting as an early warning system for risk and resource bottlenecks
- Measurement and reporting on benefits realisation
- Providing fit for purpose project delivery frameworks

Visibility & clarity

The purpose of an EPMO is to align strategically with the organisation and provide holistic management and oversight over multiple program streams.

As a conduit between those streams and the executive, the EPMO should provide visibility for corporate executives for in-flight projects and projects. The EPMO is more likely to receive continuous support from the executive team if it provides clear and accurate visibility on the status of projects and programs.

The benefits to Project Managers on the ground is that the challenges and issue they face can get executive airtime and thus top down decision making can occur through EPMO support.

The EPMO as an early warning system to prevent centralised shared service bottle necks. EPMO reporting can provide clarity on program and group wide risks, resource constraints, and potential conflicts on the demands on people and infrastructure.

Centralised shared services on the other hand often do not have visibility of what the resource requirements will be and when they will be required by projects. By the time they know it, it's already too late and they have to play catch up to meet the demands causing delays.

Early visibility of schedules and requirements enables a group wide view and a deeper understanding of what resources and infrastructure will be needed in the short, medium and longer term. Not having this view leads to project delays and eventually project failure.

Benefits realisation

EPMOs can add significant value by regular and constant monitoring of the benefits realisation of programs and projects. Tracking benefits (based on good business cases) ensures that projects actually do deliver on their promises.

Fit for purpose project delivery frameworks

EPMOs can provide significant value to project delivery by providing fit for purpose delivery frameworks (templates, processes, governance structures etc.) that compliment an organisation's delivery DNA.

The successful EPMO should be a capability centre for the project managers that help them set up their projects for success and support the project through all the phases to delivery.

Working across the entire organisation

Ensuring that portfolio, program and project execution remains aligned with business needs and drivers requires a holistic viewpoint that strategically aligned EPMOs can provide.

In its conduit role, an EPMO can provide real value to project managers and the business when it links individual streams of work to insightful, crisp reporting and fit for purpose delivery frameworks.

This helps set up projects for success and provides clear visibility to the executive of what is being achieved, identifies risks and enables effective resource management.

The role of PMO in Project Manager Capability Uplift

What are the best options to increase your Project Manager's capability?

Project managers require a diverse set of skills to successfully deliver projects, and more often than not, most will invest time and effort in continuous learning to ensure they stay abreast of new project methodologies, to enhance their skill set and to grow their knowledge.

In 2011, researchers from Chalmers University of Technology, Sweden, conducted a study of technology PMOs to understand why PMOs are established and the scope of their responsibilities.

The study showed that PMOs could deliver better projects, save time and money – and possibly the sanity of many stakeholders – by investing in project-related competence and cross-project learning for their PMs.

It begs the question: if you want to increase the capability of your project teams, specifically project managers, what are the best options available to a PMO?

Define what a Project Managers skill set should be

The PMBOK 10 Knowledge Areas are a good reference to ensure the basics are in place with your PMs and a good yardstick to assess their capability.

The 10 knowledge areas are:

1. Integration Management
2. Scope Management
3. Time Management
4. Cost Management
5. Quality Management
6. Human Resource Management

7. Communications Management
8. Risk Management
9. Procurement Management
10. Stakeholders Management

The first 9 areas is an essential skill for a PM to have. The 10th knowledge area has been added in the latest (5th) edition of the PMBOK Body of Knowledge.

Stakeholder management (the soft skills of project delivery) is a most welcome addition because if you get everything else right but fail with the stakeholder management the project will suffer.

Whichever options you consider with regards to capability uplifting of your PMs, stakeholder management – and specifically people skills – is a vital component that should not be overlooked.

Let's explore some of the options available to PMOs when considering how to build capability within their project teams.

Formal offsite training

For junior PMs or BAs that show interest and capability to become a PM, getting fundamental knowledge of a project methodology can be very helpful.

The specific methodology is up to the PMO and should be referenced against what is required within your organisation to deliver projects successfully.

Each methodology (Prince II, PMBOK, Agile etc.) has its place and provide structure, tools and a disciplined approach to project management.

However, steps should be taken to ensure the fundamentals of the selected training course will align well with the organisations delivery approach.

Bespoke, company specific training

Engaging a specialist training organisation to come in, assess your needs and build a specific course or series of courses can often deliver greater value.

Bringing outside training skills in means the organisation can use and enhance existing templates, cover company specific examples of lessons learnt and review internal successes, which add relevant context and can be applied directly to the project delivery environment PMs find themselves in.

Bringing in senior (external) capability to mentor and guide PMs

Bringing in a guru as a program manager/ project director with extensive experience in successful delivery is a great way for PMs to learn by osmosis.

As great as training courses can be, there is nothing quite as educational as being a part of a difficult situation and seeing how someone else deals with it successfully first hand. Even better?

Allowing a team to fail first then receiving supportive and constructive feedback to ensure success a second time will help PMs learn from failure as much as successes.

Gradual increase in complexity of Projects

Larger organisations that have a steady stream of projects of different sizes and complexity have an opportunity to progress and stretch their PMs as they grow and evolve.

Selecting the rising stars to take on a bigger and more complex project will not only enable them to develop their skills but also give them challenges so they don't go stale and leave the company.

Similarly, the organisation can support and mentor those that are not evolving as quickly by "safely" exposing them to how program managers and project directors manage complexity.

Stakeholder management capability uplift

The 10th knowledge area of PMBOK (Stakeholder Management) is arguably the most important area to develop and grow an organisation's PMs.

Empathy, communication and imagination are all the staples of effective stakeholder engagement. Stakeholder management development is not straightforward and formal training can help, as well as working alongside seasoned PMs.

However often the best way for PMs to learn stakeholder management is on the job. Particularly partnering them with challenging stakeholders and then monitoring and providing support and feedback as required.

Key attributes for successful PMs

Certain attributes are essential to maximise the success of your PMs, not least of which is self-belief and the ability to cope well with uncertainty. These are not easy skills to teach and are often the result of a well-rounded personal and professional life.

PMs who strive to possess an appropriate level of self-belief – to back themselves and their team – can go a long way.

Those needing a little inspiration might find it in an oft-quoted prayer from Reinhold Niebuhr: "Grand me the strength to accept the things I cannot change, the courage to change the things I can and the wisdom to know the difference."

The ability to cope with uncertainty is also critical – which is a trait developed over time and often coupled with the development of resilience.

Coping with uncertainty requires the ability to make sense of different and often complex options, articulate complicated ideas in an easily understood manner and the flexibility to adapt the approach, behaviour and planning whilst keeping an eye on the agreed final outcomes.

Enablement and empowerment – Developing soft skills

Soft skills are usually life skills that aren't taught as part of a formal project management course. It's these areas that PMOs can get creative in how they develop their project managers.

Non-project management courses can round out a PM and provide real benefits, such as building confidence, learning how to develop rapport, enhancing writing and communication skills and self-awareness.

Most important are the courses and training that enable PMs to be transparent and have the confidence to deliver news, irrespective of whether it is good or bad.

One of Quay's key mantras is that '… there is no good news or bad news – only news.' It takes a strong, experienced and well-supported project manager to live that mantra.

Enterprise & Technology PMOs: The Visible Differences

How is an Enterprise PMO (EPMO) different to Technology PMO?

There is often confusion about the primary purpose of a Program Management Office and why it exists within an organisation.

- Is it there for tools, processes and capability uplift only?
- Is it there to manage, allocate and mentor the pool of project resources?
- Or is it there to manage, inform and finalise the investment portfolio for an organisation?

The truth is no PMO is the same and most will have some of the above within their remit of responsibilities.

Typically, the level of service provided by a PMO will more often than not be dictated by two key variables; the project delivery maturity of the organisation and more importantly where the PMO sits within the organisation.

It is the later point that we explore below, in particular, what are the differences between an Enterprise PMO (EPMO) that sits across the entire business versus a PMO that sits exclusively within Technology?

(For the purposes of this discussion, we are excluding any analysis on the Program PMO, which is a PMO set up for an individual, discreet initiative.)

EPMOs focus on the strategic investment portfolio

The EPMO should have a top-down approach when assessing the portfolio of projects to deliver.

Given the organisation wide remit of an EPMO, the focus will be on the overall strategic investment portfolio and the alignment of the project portfolio to this strategic vision. The EPMO will seek to advance the overall organisation's goals not just individual silos.

Typically, a Technology PMO will have a bottom-up approach when assessing the project slate, with a focus on the tactical and thus lack the EPMO's strategic alignment.

The focus within a Technology PMO then often becomes more about doing projects "right" as opposed to doing "the right projects" for the overall good of the organisation.

EPMOs are about transformation

EPMOs have a focus across the whole business and delivery of the overall strategy which leads to EPMO initiatives typically being more transformational than a Technology PMO.

EPMOs have a focus across the whole business and delivery of the overall strategy which leads to EPMO initiatives typically being more transformational than a Technology PMO.

The greater focus on transformational projects and programs being managed by an EPMO means the projects often have significant business impacts.

As a result, EPMOs need far greater focus on managing business change within the portfolio of projects.

The heightened change requirements for an EPMO portfolio requires that the EPMO be well versed in change management fundamentals, tools and processes to ensure it can support the delivery teams as required and also be a champion of change management with the key stakeholders.

EPMOs face into the business stakeholders

Given their strategic focus, EPMOs will face back into the business, which brings its own unique challenges.

For example, the majority of the stakeholders are usually C-level and often pressed for time (yes – it's true).

They also may not have as sound a grasp of project fundamentals and disciplines as technology stakeholders do, since the latter's day-to-day focus is more project orientated than their business counterparts.

In the strategic position they hold, EPMO managers need to be very good at managing stakeholders, highly skilled in communication and well versed in managing upwards with a focus on educating the audience on project delivery fundamentals.

An EPMO can drive standardisation across a business

With its whole-of-business remit, an EPMO has a golden opportunity to drive standardisation of project delivery across the entire organisation, not just within technology.

Their role could include mandating standardisation of templates (reporting, business cases etc.), governance structures, approval processes, influencing selection of methodologies (Agile, Iterative Waterfall etc.), benefits management, scope management, risk and issue management.

An EPMO can also take steps to centralising the resource pools for the overall benefit of the portfolio planning and delivery.

Whilst the above list is not exhaustive it does call out some of the more visible differences between an EPMO and the traditional Technology PMO.

Both certainly have their place within an organisation but they are nuanced and require different skills sets to establish and manage.

In the perfect world they actually can learn and leverage off each other in the pursuit of better overall project outcomes, which is the reason they are both established in the first place.

CHAPTER 7
MANAGING ORGANISATIONAL CHANGE

Why is change the first casualty of war?

Managing change is difficult at the best of times, but focusing only on technology solutions without the discipline of business change management may limit real success.

Managing change is difficult at the best of times, but focusing only on technology solutions without the discipline of business change management may limit real success.

Projects often fail because of the inability of the project team to effectively manage the change – be it new technology or processes - into the business. Ensuring that change execution is part of the strategy from the outset – not a 'nice-to-have' or an afterthought – can significantly impact the success of your project's execution.

Strategy, tactics and rising above the noise

The eloquent technical delivery of a solution is all well and good, however if not accompanied with robust fit-for-purpose change management then the overall project may fail to achieve the critical KPI of business take up and acceptance.

Change management is an ongoing blind spot in projects, particularly those with a technical emphasis, and there are a myriad of reasons as to why it is often neglected or poorly executed.

Change is difficult to execute well and it can be challenging to understand the 'why' and the 'how' for many project participants.

Sun Zhu wrote that '… strategy without tactics is the slowest route to victory. Tactics without strategy is the noise before defeat.'[i] Applying the concept of strategic change management from the outset ensures that the symbiotic nature of change and technical implementation is planned for and remains intact throughout the project's delivery.

Plan for change from the outset to ensure success

It is important the change aspects of any project are given due consideration up front and suitably planned for and resourced appropriately.

Below are a number of actions project managers and sponsors should be considering when approaching their projects and traps they would do well to avoid.

It is never technology for technology's sake

The underlying technology of a project should be viewed as the key enabler.

But for the project to be successful overall the change the new technology brings must be managed so that the business understand, accept and can adapt to their new work practices to unlock the functionality and benefits of any technology changes.

Change is not just comms

Change is often misunderstood and reduced to just a communications work stream. Whilst communication is critical it is just one of the key streams of any change program.

Real change must identify the gap between how the business currently operates and how they need to operate effectively in the new world.

Just telling the business about what is coming does not take into account what they may need to change to be able to do their jobs in the future.

Change is not just training

Ditto the above!

Never assume what is easy and what is hard for the business

Nobody knows their business better than the people within it. Many projects fail through lack of investing in change or failing to bring people on board and the project team are left making assumptions about what impacts a change may bring.

This plays out negatively on two fronts. Firstly by assuming what may be required for the business to adapt to change things can be missed or understated which impacts roll out and sustained take up.

Secondly the business can become hostile toward the project if the project team have paid little or no attention to their real needs through poor change engagement. This can play out through on-going animosity between the business and the project.

Select the right project leaders

Make sure when resourcing the key roles for the project team that the people targeted understand the importance of change and know that projects need both excellent technical execution and change execution to be successful overall.

Often the 'technical' is the project manager's comfort zone which can manifest in a lack of focus on the business impact and change requirements for a project.

An easy test is to have any potential project leader's walk through what a change strategy document should look like in terms of the table of contents and the intent of such a document.

Maintain the balance between change management and technical solution

There is no question the change stream of any project is often the most nuanced and therefore often the most difficult capability for project members and sponsors to understand and get right.

So it is important that the easy option is not taken by reducing the focus to the technical.

The technical and change implementation have a symbiotic relationship. If the project is to be considered an overall success then good technical execution must always be accompanied by excellent change disciplines and change should not become a nice-to-have or an afterthought.

Developing the right change strategy

How can an organisation ensure that it is consistently choosing the right projects as part of its change strategy?

For an organisation to run a consistently successful change program it should be focused on three fundamental objectives:

- Is the organisation doing the right projects?
- At the right time?
- In the right way?

The last two objectives are disciplines very familiar to all project professionals: portfolio management and project delivery.

However the first objective, 'doing the right projects', is more often than not well beyond the influence of project managers and it is here sub-standard investment decisions can be made off the back of poorly developed strategy. But how can an organisation take steps to ensure its strategy is fit for purpose at any given point in time and therefore the project slate being delivered is the right one for effecting change?

This is not easy but there are a number of actions a change executive can take, or risks to be mindful of, to ensure success.

Create an effective, repeatable forum to develop the strategy

Finite resources – in particular, money – determine which projects are prioritised, as no organisation can implement every project opportunity.

A suitable forum must therefore be established with the right people and tools to enable strategy to be developed with a sufficient amount of critical thinking going into the project selection process to ensure it is fit for purpose. The process also needs to repeatable, not a one off.

He who shouts loudest should not always get the money

Developing strategy is by its very nature a competitive process. When strategies are being developed, it's important that self-interest is taken out of the equation.

The people responsible for delivering the strategy need to think and operate as a collective for the greater good of the organisation and prioritise projects accordingly.

Always applying oil to the squeaky wheel is not necessarily the best use of an organisation's finite project delivery capability.

Flexibility is good but...

Strategies should not remain static, as they need to evolve to meet changing business environments.

However if they change too frequently there will be an adverse impact on the organisation's ability to deliver projects. Nothing disrupts an organisation's delivery capability more than continually chopping-and-changing project priorities.

A process and timetable needs to be developed that ensures the strategy can be flexible but not at the expense of continually disrupting the in-flight project slate.

Make the connection between strategy and project delivery

Whoever is ultimately responsible for strategy should have a very good understanding of what is required to prioritise and then deliver the projects to meet the strategy's objectives.

Some projects are too ambitious at a point in time and perhaps cannot be delivered or need to be broken down and executed over a longer period than the strategy allows.

The organisation can save a significant amount of planning time, or project churn, if those responsible for the strategy have a very good understanding of the organisations project delivery processes and the organisations project delivery limitations.

A constant challenge

Developing and maintaining a relevant strategy that will meet an organisation's goals is a continual challenge.

This should never be done in isolation without a good understanding of the project delivery capability and capacity.

The above list is not exhaustive but is an indicator of where attention should be focused to help ensure an organisation is always doing the right projects, at the right time in the right way.

Embedding organisational change management for success

A critical way to ensure that IT's value as a business partner is acknowledged is to successfully deliver business projects.

While project management is a vital part of successful project delivery, embedding change management into the delivery of projects can increase the chances of a successful outcome by up to six times (*Prosci Benchmarking Report, 2011ⁱⁱ*).

Why change management matters

While project management focuses on the discipline of delivering the technical, administrative and functional aspects of business projects, change management focuses on the people (business) side of project delivery. Embedding change into projects prepares the business for the transition from "how we do things now" to "how we will do things in the future." Engaging people in the process of change is critical to ensuring a successful outcome.

Why are projects approved by a business?

Projects are approved by organisations to achieve improvements in performance (in one way or another) by making changes to processes, systems, tools, job roles and organisational structures which ultimately require individuals to change how they do their jobs (in almost all cases).

If the people within the business are not engaged and encouraged to take this last step, then the opportunity for success is lost.

According to Posci's change management learning centre, the number one obstacle to success is employee resistance.

In *Putting the Business Back into the Business Case*, we explored some of the key ways that IT departments risk their existence by ignoring business partnering opportunities, rather than becoming a key enabler and business partner. Failing to bring people on board for the project is tantamount to risking its success.

Embedding change requires a strategic outlook from the get-go to ensure that the most vital cog of change – people – is brought along for the journey.

Steps to Embed Change

According to Prosci, the steps to ensure IT projects engage the business (people) through change management and deliver the benefits to the business (as a strong strategic partner) are listed below:

1. It starts from the top with strong and effective sponsorship from senior leaders.
2. Get the right people in the right places to ensure appropriate and fit-for-purpose resourcing.
3. Engage the business with "what's in it for me" through clear articulation and communication on the benefits for individuals, teams and the organisation.
4. Get engagement/buy-in from individuals, teams and the organisation by listening to and supporting the business concerns from all stakeholders across the business.
5. "Show, don't just tell' – Excellent communication in all its forms (actions, behaviour, spoken, written, group and individual) need to demonstrate how change will benefit the business.
6. Be aligned – strong alignment between project managers and change managers is essential to ensure they are rowing the same boat.
7. Facilitate action and feedback by hearing concerns, taking action and soliciting continual feedback.

As a strategic partner to your business, IT cannot afford to overlook the need for change management in projects.

Embedding change using the above 7 steps will start you on the road to successfully engaging the business (people) and set your projects up for success.

A project team wide approach to delivering change

Managing change successfully is more often than not the most challenging aspect of any business or technology project.

Delivering successful change can rarely be achieved satisfactorily via a paint-by-numbers approach.

Each project has its own unique change challenges and it often requires a nuanced approach to be successful. The techniques that worked for previous projects may not be appropriate for future projects as each business change is different.

Furthermore, the change responsibilities often fall to a single individual change manager who may be covering an impacted user population in the hundreds or even thousands.

Given this relationship dynamic of one-to-many how can a change manager better leverage the project team to help deliver successful change?

Make all team members change champions

Project team members are a valuable asset in delivering change, mainly because they are in constant contact with user groups being affected by change.

Where possible project team members, in particular business-facing personnel such as business analysts, should be used to explain and promote business change during their interaction with those user groups.

Project team members need to be identified and engaged so that they fully understand the reason for change, the benefits of change and the change approach. This will help to mitigate against potentially adverse business impacts.

Project team members are at the coalface: they will be faced with constant questions about what the changes will mean to user groups.

As change champions, they will need to be equipped with the correct change information but more importantly, they also need to understand their greater responsibility to the project in helping deliver change.

Use the project team to gain insights

Taking an ivory tower approach to gathering information and planning changes is usually detrimental to effective implementation of change.

Be prepared to utilise your project team to help capture information that may be of use to the change approach being implemented.

The change manager should be actively establishing the right relationships within the team from the start and setting up regular forums to gather, review and validate insights that allow the change approach to be measured on an ongoing basis.

They are on the ground; they know what will work

Once the relationships with the project team members are established, the change manager should be prepared to listen.

The team members are the boots on the ground for the project. They can often be spending significant amounts of time with or embedded in the business.

Whilst they may not be trained in change management they will be a very good source of information as to what will work due to their insights into the user groups.

Adapt the change approach as appropriate

Like a project, the successful delivery of change can be a journey of discovery. Once the insights have been captured and validated, the change manager should be willing to adjust the approach to delivering the change as required.

Rigid, fixed thinking can limit the execution of successful change so be prepared to take the information gathered by the team during the life of the project to adapt the change approach as required to increase the chances of success.

Ensure you have substance, not just technical style

Ultimately the success of any project is greatly dependent on the effectiveness of the change effort. An eloquent technical implementation is not enough if not accompanied by good change management.

So it remains in the best interests of all project team members that the change is delivered effectively.

The change manager should harness this dynamic wherever possible to expand the pool of potential change resources at their disposal and set up the relationships in such a way that they get full benefit of this expanded change team.

Do PMs also need to be Change Managers to be successful?

Typically, when projects are being introduced or undertaken within an organisation, change occurs.

It's often only the type of change and the size or scale of change that varies between projects. But not all project budgets stretch far enough to include a stand-alone change manager and this requirement can often be overlooked anyway.

The question then is do all project managers need some change skills to be successful?

Before we dive into the roles and responsibilities of a project manager, let's set the context of what a project actually is.

The definition of a 'project'

In defining what a project looks like, it's helpful to look at some theory as defined by the Project Management Institute from *A Guide to the Project Management Body of Knowledge* (PMBOK Guide, Fifth Edition (2013)).

The PMI defines a project as being a temporary endeavour designed to produce a unique product, service or result with a defined beginning and end – usually time-constrained and often constrained by funding or deliverables – undertaken to meet unique goals and objectives, typically to bring about beneficial change or added value.

From this we know that a project delivers change so managing that change will be a critical enabler of success for the project.

Differentiating project management and change management

Once we understand what constitutes a project, the next step is to understand project management.

In short, project management is the process and activity of planning, organising, motivating and controlling resources, procedures and protocols to achieve specific goals.

A project manager undertakes the planning, monitoring and controlling of the project from inception to closure.

The PMBOK tells us this is done through five main processes (initiating, planning, executing, monitoring and controlling and closing) and ten knowledge areas.

Each of the ten knowledge areas contains the processes that need to be accomplished within its discipline in order to achieve effective project management. Each of these processes also falls into one of the five process groups, creating a matrix structure such that every process can be related to one knowledge area and one process group.

So what is Change Management?

Change management is an approach to transitioning individuals, teams, and organisations to a desired future state. In a project management context, change management may also refer to a project management process wherein changes to the scope of a project are formally introduced and approved.

Change management is an integral part of project management

Put simply Change Management is an integral part of Project Management – be it managing the change in the context of the project deliverables such as time, cost, quality, scope and benefits (Project Change) or managing the change into the stakeholder community i.e. those people impacted by the change the project brings (Stakeholder Change).

But does this mean the Project Manager has to also be the Change Manager?

A rule of thumb would be the higher number of affected stakeholders from a project the greater the need for a specialist Change Manager to manage the change to the stakeholder community i.e. Stakeholder Change. The Project Manager will still manage the Project Change.

Change Management has developed significantly as a profession over recent years with a number of leading methodologies for delivering change.

A Change Management methodology provides a disciplined process for managing the change into the stakeholders being used i.e. Prosci, is a market leading methodology.

Integrating change into project management

In summary then, a Project Manager – whether managing the Stakeholder Change or simply managing delivering the Project – must recognize that Change Management is a critical success enabler and have tasks and activities assigned accordingly.

Understanding the effects and providing for impacts on stakeholders is crucial to delivering a positive outcome from the project.

Within the Ten Knowledge Areas there are two obvious areas that can be attributed to Change Management namely Communications Management and Stakeholder Management:

Communications Management – Project Communications Management includes the processes that are required to ensure timely and appropriate planning, collection, creation, distribution, storage, retrieval, management, control, monitoring, and the ultimate disposition of project information.

Stakeholder Management – Project Stakeholder Management includes the processes required to identify all people or organizations impacted by the project, analysing stakeholder expectations and impact on the project, and developing appropriate management strategies for effectively engaging stakeholders in project decisions and execution.

So do your PMs need to be Change Managers as well?

Quay's view is that this can be a grey area that must take into account many factors, but none more so than project complexity.

Project Managers need basic change management skills but the question needs to be asked whether change management can be executed successfully by the PM or whether the project is sufficiently complex and the depth of change required warrants the engagement of a professional Change Manager.

Successfully blending business change with technical delivery

What are the factors at play that project managers and teams need to be mindful of when delivering business change alongside technical delivery?

Without doubt one of the most difficult aspects for any project to consistently get right is how to embed a technical solution successfully into the business.

Exceptional technical delivery by itself is no guarantee of project success if it is not accompanied by an equally effective business change process.

There are a number of factors at play that make this final, but critical component of project success difficult to achieve.

Below we examine some potential pitfalls that project managers and project teams should be aware of when striving for excellence - not only in technical delivery but also in embedding business change.

The never-ending horizon

Implementing the change into the business is more or less the last thing to occur on a project.

With many projects typically running for more than 12 months, the final business change activities can often appear remote and far off in the distance.

The full extent of the challenge of the business change can be neglected during the initial scoping and planning of a project due to the long timelines with the focus on the more immediate technical activities.

To get the jump on what successful business change activities will be required and to facilitate some meaningful, early planning, the project manager should set aside time to review past implementations, for example:

- Talk to other PMs who have delivered change in that particular business area
- Review lessons learned from PIRs etc.

They should also engage early not only with the business sponsor but also the subject matter experts (SMEs): those people who will be on the ground during any deployment, throughout the planning phases.

This should give the project manager better insights into what will be required and allow for these business change activities to be catered for in early scoping and planning exercises.

What else is going on?

Good project managers by definition can be indifferent to the world around them as they pursue the successful delivery of their scope.

Whilst they may understand (and be able to feign genuine concern!) for other projects and business challenges around them what they are really about is driving the outcomes of their project.

This single-minded focus is a prerequisite of any project manager as it is the delivery of their scope they will be held to account for. However, such a myopic approach can also come at a cost, particularly when planning successful business change.

Project managers should be open to investigating early in the planning process what other business change is planned for in their impacted business units, including what business challenges they may be facing into the future (headcount reductions, changing business landscapes etc).

Such information will help inform the planning process for the business change activities and guard against inaccurate assumptions being made that may impact the project later in its lifecycle.

Spend some quality time with the business

Too often project managers spend most their time with the technical staff on their projects. This could be triaging issues, reviewing the technical plans, assisting with the planning and execution of testing cycles etc.

This focus on the technical can come at a cost. It does not begin to provide the end user insights that are required to ensure the technical changes can be embedded successfully into the business.

If project managers were to change this focus and begin to devote a greater percentage of their time engaged with the business, the insights gained should greatly increase their appreciation of the business change challenges and ensure better planning and execution of this business change.

The types of things a project manager could do include spending a day on the front line with the users, floor walking with the SMEs and meeting the influencers personally within the business teams. They should also be attending team meetings as an observer to better understand the user group dynamics.

All of these activities should provide the project manager better insights into how the business unit ticks and these insights could then be factored into the business change activities.

Delivering successful business change requires accurate insights

The points above are by no means exhaustive. Delivering successful business change is complex and forever challenging and requires the right inputs (i.e. accurate insights) for project managers to plan successfully. It cannot be wholly outsourced to the change manager.

The project manager has a responsibility to provide whatever assistance they can to set the change effort up for success and by following some of the suggestions above, the business change has a greater chance of matching and complimenting the success of any technical delivery.

Assessing the success of change management

How do you know your change management has been successful?

When organisations complete projects, it is critical that its success – or failure – is captured and measured. Learning the lessons from past projects (both negative and positive) can help drive better execution into the future and also validate for a project delivery team and change executive that they are on the right track.

Measuring change and success

Measuring the success or otherwise of the technical delivery aspects of a project can be relatively straightforward.

The key measures like time, cost and critical functionality can be easy to identify and track whether success has been achieved. However an eloquent technical implementation does not always translate into a successful project unless it is matched with equally effective business engagement and change management activities.

The measurement of success of these change management activities is less straightforward and can be neglected during post implementations reviews (PIRs).

Often the change management activities are difficult to link to easily identifiable or quantifiable success measures and as such are either excluded from PIRs or the capture of them is ineffective.

Below are some steps that can be taken to ensure during a project review the execution of the change management activities are also suitably captured and analysed:

Cast the net wide

It is not always immediately apparent who in the business is affected downstream by a projects technical or business process changes.

Take the time to work with the business to understand and identify who may be impacted beyond the immediate user group and ensure they are included in the PIR process as appropriate.

More is more

Once these users have been identified, err on the side of excess. Include as many of the impacted users along the chain as possible in any review process to get as wide a range of responses as can be achieved.

Often users will not respond but typically no news is good news and paints a picture of the success of the project in itself. Either way users will appreciate being included even if they do not take the time to respond.

Use technology to your advantage

Cost and time constraints (on both sides) and also geography mean not everyone can be interviewed one on one. Furthermore large workshops with the business can often be difficult to manage and not necessarily be the right forum for people to speak up, particularly if it is in the negative.

An effective way to gather large quantities of data across disparate and often large user groups is online surveys. These surveys should be designed so the information is easy to understand and collated once the responses are submitted.

Ask the right questions

The project team should be open to all findings, whether negative or positive, and the survey questions should be structured accordingly.

Change management is not an exact science so ensure the surveys allow for the users to include a rating so they can express how they feel they were engaged beyond a simple 'yes' or 'no'. Allow for a free text field of reasonable length at the end of the survey with a request that any further information be added.

Follow up directly on any feedback that needs clarification. Also ask how things could have been done better or improved.

It is these responses that will add the most value and build up the project team's change management IP for the next project.

Capturing the impact of change

Change management is not an exact science and every organisation and user group has a differing ability to absorb change. By following some of the above suggestions the effectiveness of any change effort can be captured and accurately assessed.

Future change activities can then be modified appropriately to increase the chances of the project being a business change success and not just a technical one.

CHAPTER 8
THE RISE OF BIG DATA AND DIGITAL

Key insights for successfully implementing digital strategies

Who are the key players in the Australian project management industry?

Businesses are moving steadily towards the adoption of Digital within their organisations, and the emergence of the Chief Digital Officer has signaled that Digital needs to take its rightful place within overall business strategy.

Executing this digital take-up is not without its challenges. The main focus for organisations is to understand how Digital is impacting business, what constitutes 'critical success' and the organisational implications of integrating Digital strategy into the business.

Below we've outlined a number of insights that we believe will help organisations to better plan for, implement and measure success of Digital.

Insight 1: What do you mean by 'Digital'?

When defining your Digital strategy, there are many interpretations of what 'Digital' means – and all would be right.

'Digital' has become an all encompassing term that for business can include the Internet; cloud-based service delivery; digital automation of business processes; customer interaction and engagement via online marketing or social media; mobile applications for tablets and smartphones; and big data, not to mention the ability to embrace mobility for your workforce.

To help organisations with this conversation, we distill Digital into three key categories:

- Providing new products and services to customers
- Enhancing existing products and services with Digital
- Process improvement, be it re-engineering, replacing and integrating Digital into the mix

Insight 2: Integrating Digital strategy into overall business strategy

The second insight is that businesses must ensure that Digital strategy for each category is integrated into overall business strategy to enable it to succeed. For example:

- New products strategy – to create a new customer product (New)
- Enhanced customer strategy – to offer existing Digital content in a tablet or mobile format (Existing)
- Efficient strategy – to create automated workflow for procurement (Process)

Insight 3: Organisational structure and delivery models + Digital

Our third insight is that an organisation's structure and delivery models need to compliment the integration of the Digital strategy into the business.

For example, does the organisational structure and delivery model lend itself to:

- 'Experimental' delivery and a skunkworks style autonomy with an agile management style? (New)
- Digital being one element within an overall solution, what works best within existing structures? (Enhance)
- Digital being one element within an overall solution, what can be improved with digital integration? (Improve).

Insight 4: The cultural divide

The fourth insight is a very important one, because with the introduction of a 'skunk works' delivery team there is potential for a cultural divide to appear.

Skunk works appeared as a term during the Second World War by engineers working at Lockheed, where a team of engineers where tasked with developing a fighter jet with minimal management constraints. In project delivery via a skunk works style approach, there needs to be awareness of an 'us and them' culture that may unfold within the business between digital staff and the rest of your staff.

This is because:

- Digital staff tend to be younger, less 'business' experienced and more experimental than traditional staff (both in the business and IT), which can result in a clash of cultures.
- The freedom and autonomy offered to skunkworks-style teams can and does create an 'us-and-them' divide with the rest of the organisation, so care needs to be taken to position and integrate the outputs back into the business.

Without the business-buy-in, the outputs run the real risk of become shelf ware.

Insight 5: C-suite sponsorship is vital

The final and by no means least important insight is that for Digital initiatives to be successful they must have C-suite sponsorship and actives support.

This provides a means to:

- Position the Digital within the context of the organisation's overall strategy
- Foster collaboration effectively across the organisation
- Drive business buy-in to outputs generated from Digital teams

The upshot of these insights is that the integration of Digital into business strategy is complex, as its tethers can reach far and deep into the organisation.

However, despite that complexity, there are numerous advantages to integrating digital. The challenge is to ensure that your business is set up for success from the outset.

Structuring a digital program for success

How can a business better define and communicate the context of digital programs within their organisation?

Digital programs are quintessentially no different from any typical program undertaken by most organizations, yet while the fundamentals of Program and Project Management typically hold true, there's always a "but".

In our experience, that "but" comes from the struggle many digital programs have in effectively positioning themselves with respect to exactly what the digital operating model is and how it integrates within the broader context of the organization.

This lack of positioning and definition leads to unnecessary tension between digital, other business and IT stakeholders.

So how can you avoid this tension? We've outlined four steps for ensuring you set up digital programs for success.

Step One: Define the context

As we wrote in Key Insights for Successfully Implementing Digital Strategies (Aug 2013) the word "digital" has become an all-encompassing term for business that can include:

- The creating of a digital business unit offering products and services
- The Internet
- Cloud-based service delivery
- Digital automation of business processes
- Customer interaction and engagement via online marketing or social media
- Mobile applications for tablets and smart phones
- Big data

Add to that the ability to embrace mobility for your workforce and it's easy to see how "digital" can be misinterpreted or misunderstood.

The first step in avoiding the tension that can be created is to define and communicate effectively what "digital" means in the context of both the program and the organisation.

To help organisations with this conversation, we distill Digital into three key categories:

- Providing new products and services to customers
- Enhancing existing products and services with Digital
- Process improvement, be it re-engineering, replacing and integrating Digital into the mix

Step Two: Define the Operating Model i.e. Business Integration

Where many programs struggle is gaining clarity and agreement on the business ownership model, especially where new digital products and services are developed.

Traditionally IT has been the owner of all things IT and as such digital programs would naturally fit there however when the technology is the business the lines of demarcation become blurred.

A good example is to look at Publishing.

Traditional print business models are well established with clearly defined processes and owners for Editorial, Pre-Press, Advertising, Publishing and Distribution.

IT supplies and supports the underlying systems and infrastructure to support the business processes but what happens when the publications become available in a digital format and/or new digital-only publications are produced that don't have a print-based parent?

In our experience where new Digital products and services are introduced this might create a new business unit where technology outputs are the products and/or services (i.e. the business).

We believe the following guiding principles can be used to help determine ownership and accountability of digital products and services within the organization:

IT defines the standards and technologies acceptable to be introduced into the organisation. This ensures that any technology introduced will be supportable and integrate within the enterprise environment (link: Architecture).

IT should continue to provide and support the environment including networks, servers, security, storage, desktops, internet etc. (even when provided via the cloud).

The business unit should select the digital products it wishes to use (within the constraints above) and provide the functional support of the same.

Where existing processes are simply enhanced by digital, this needs to be looked at and agreed on a case-by-case basis as to what makes sense.

Step 3: Defining Roles and Responsibilities

Digital Business may have a number of functions which in the past have naturally sat in the IT domain, for example:

- Product Developers
- Product Architects
- Digital Producers

Care needs to be taken to clearly identify these roles and agree accountabilities and responsibilities and how they interact with IT and other business owners. Where end-to-end business processes cross manual and digital boundaries, clear definition of ownership, accountability and responsibility for each step in the process is paramount.

Step 4: Defining and Communicating the Delivery Approach

As many digital initiatives naturally lend themselves to agile and innovation style delivery approaches we strongly encourage ensuring the delivery approach is well articulated, fit for purpose and stakeholder expectations managed.

Where a business is used to waterfall or iterative style delivery methods, many stakeholders struggle to understand how the projects are being funded, project managed and the ensuing benefits realisation model.

Having the awareness of this, creating and staying on message and ensuring governance, funding and procurement processes are appropriate to support the model goes a long way to minimising unnecessary stakeholder concerns.

Leverage experience and knowledge

Quay's view is that Digital Programs are not any different from any other program; they should be set-up for success with appropriate governance, delivery methodology and project management.

However, to maximise the chance of success care needs to be taken to clearly define and communicate the context of the program within the organisation, the operating model that supports the program both during and post-delivery, clearly defined roles and responsibilities (especially digital resources) and the ownership and integration of end to end business processes impacted by the program.

The digital economy: the fundamentals of digital transformation

How can your organisation build solid fundamentals for digital transformation?

It is beyond question that all organisations are now operating in the new digital economy.

The challenge to remain accessible, relevant and profitable to an ever-evolving customer base is gathering pace and complexity and the importance of getting digital transformation right – and sustainable – is paramount.

However, it is not easy to achieve digital transformation, as the new working environment is getting increasingly complex. Whilst digital transformation is not a one size fits all there are some emerging fundamentals on how to approach it that are worth noting.

These fundamentals include customer focus, acknowledging the on-going nature of digital transformation, ownership from the top, encouraging agile project delivery techniques and delivering back office innovation as part of the program.

Some of these key considerations that should be in scope when planning for a successful digital transformation are explored in more detail below:

Know thy customer

Knowledge of your customer is the foundation stone for any future digital transformation. So what do you need to really understand? The fundamentals include:

- Knowledge of how they interact with products and services
- Which platforms are they using now and may use in the future?
- Are they early adopters?

- What is their level of satisfaction?

A whole industry is emerging around capturing data to understand the Customer Experience (CX). The key is that once captured, using data analytics to discern market segmentations and trends helps organisations to develop a road map of projects to meet the customer's new requirements.

This is a very complex area and is driving the rise of the Digital Information Officer (DIO), which we will revisit in a future article.

It has to be top down

The digital transformation needs to be raised to the corporate level. In many organisations digital transformation is a bottom-up affair, which creates silos of unconnected activity and leads to both duplication of effort and also gaps appearing in digital offerings. It's the worst of both worlds.

However, the most critical impact of this lack of a common purpose is the creation of an enterprise architecture that is unsustainable and does not ultimately meet the digital needs of the organisation – now or into the future.

Elevating and then driving all digital transformations from the corporate level will reduce many of the above risks.

It's never over, even when it's over

Unlike, say, the traditional implementation of an ERP the execution of a digital transformation is an on-going activity.

Due to the constant of "change" there is no point at which an organisation can stop transforming digitally, the market dictates this is an on-going process.

Organisations will need to have the right tools and discipline to constantly monitor the effectiveness of their digital operations and have established governance structures to process and manage future changes.

Digital is also for the back office

Whilst the focus should always be first and foremost on the customer there are significant benefits to be gained from the digital transformation of internal processes as well as the customer-facing processes.

Transforming internal processes can drive down costs, increase efficiencies and create new opportunities within an organisation for better collaboration.

Create an environment to stay ahead of the game

In the new digital world the need to innovate is more critical than ever. In business success is often achieved by anticipating the market trends and becoming an early adopter of new technologies.

Use agile delivery techniques and skunkworks where appropriate to try and stay if not ahead of the curve at least keep up with it. Being innovative is critical and we have previously written about the emerging need of creating this innovative environment for your project delivery teams to operate within.

Expand your offerings

Similar to the above point on innovation don't be restricted to simply continuing to provide your current offerings.

Use your new digital platforms to investigate new products and services. Investigate potential new digital businesses and look to leverage the digital platform to reshape your organisation's boundaries.

Digital transformation is still evolving

Whilst the above list is not exhaustive it does provide a solid foundation of the critical characteristics of successful digital transformation. We would also recommend you read widely on the topic as we here at Quay do. Digital transformation is still in the process of being properly understood by all players in the market.

There are lots of resources out there, some not always accurate, but for more in depth information we recommend some of the analysis that is currently coming out of Cap Gemini.

Big Data and the digital footprint

Rather than focusing on the elusive 'data scientist', organisations do well instead to bring broader skillsets into contextualising Big Data for their projects.

We live in a world that is increasingly digital and there are few transactions or interactions in modern life that don't leave some form of digital footprint. Our activity in business, personal and social transactions is not only changing how we live - it also yields significant amounts of data, which is fuelling the digital transformation of business.

According to a recent US study, The State of Big Data Infrastructure: Benchmarking Global Big Data Users to Drive Future Performance[iii] (April 2015, Vanson Bourne), the amount of data organisations have has increased by an average of 16 percent in the last two years and is predicted to rise by a further 24 percent in the next two years. But data in and of itself tells us very little – it is ultimately the context that yields information.

Data and context must work together

A great way to illustrate the importance of context for data is to think of footprints on a beach. Each footprint tells us that people were on the beach which, in essence, is just data.

To give the data meaning, we need to look at the context of how that data came about, or how the footprints were made.

The volume of people on the beach that day and the individual characteristics about those people (height, weight, size of footprint, how deep they are etc.) are factors that provide context for how those footprints were made.

The illustration shows us that the footprints by themselves only tell us that people were on the beach; however it's the contextual information that will help us derive understanding and meaning about the behaviour of people.

To gain information, you need to add context and value to the data. The relationship between Big Data and Digital, it is the platform (i.e. the beach) allows us to gather a wide array of data (i.e. footprints), but it's the context that gives it meaning.

So what is the lure of Big Data and why do our footprints matter?

The relationship between Big Data and Digital

Let's get a baseline on what Big Data and Digital are.

Big Data is an aggregation of our online history, including how we navigate, shop, search and behave online. It is a rich collection of information about how we interact with organisations, with each other and that provides a deep reservoir of data that has implications, opportunities and – in some cases – dilemmas for the marriage of Big Data and Digital.

Digital, in this context, is the method by which our footprint is recorded. "Digital" is the smartphone, the tablet, the Internet, social media and many other forms of engagement that have become – for many of us – part of the daily norm.

Our behaviour online is trackable and that is a contract many of us either unwittingly make or accept knowing that there are benefits to having a better or more convenient user experience.

The consumer perspective

A consumer's perspective may be 'where I go is my business' yet we live in the paradox of wanting anonymity online while at the same time wanting the convenience or perceived benefits of a personalised experience that delivers the information we want or need.

The perceived benefit is a significantly improved user experience, a reduction in time spent filtering non-relevant information and a reduced advertisement-to-sale timescale.

Where it gets uncomfortable is the knowledge that our individual footprints become an information asset for the collector of that data;

intelligence which can be sold on to third parties that may or may not have our best interests at heart.

For business, it can present a conundrum – how to meet the privacy and personal security expectations of customers while at the same time delivering a better service?

The business of Big Data

In the study mentioned above, many organisations see Big Data as an important facet to digital transformation and perceive Big Data to be critical for strategic business goals, such as increasing revenue, new market development and improving the customer journey.

For the organisations surveyed, most were already experiencing or anticipating that they could deliver more effective, targeted marketing and sales campaigns, increased revenue and a better understanding of how to engage with their customers.

The study identified five top issues for organisations to overcome to successfully deliver Big Data project implementation:

- Insufficient infrastructure
- Organisational Complexity
- Security, compliance and governance concerns
- Insufficient budgets and resources
- A lack of visibility into information and processes due to absent or limited capability.

The ever-increasing volume and complexity of real-time data sets are proving to be a challenge for business on many levels, however the study showed that some 84 percent of businesses surveyed saw benefits outweighing the challenges.

One of the challenges of Big Data projects is too often the focus is on the platform for the analysis, machine learning and systematising process, however the missing ingredient is also that it's about solving problems, discovering patterns within the business (and for its customers) and finding the right solutions for those problems – and upskilling your teams is just as vital.

Data Science – the missing link or a Big Data Unicorn?

Despite having plenty of data at its disposal, a business may struggle to extract the valuable nuggets from the mountain of information it has about its customers and operations due to the lack of skills within the team to do so. The platforms exist to collect and silo data, however there need to be the skill sets in the business to interpret it, distil into insights and deploy actionable strategy.

A recent study from Accenture flagged the ability to understand statistics, machine learning, sound visualisation skills and being able to design experiments to test the quality and integrity of the data as a major challenge for most businesses.

It is not insurmountable however and it's possible to utilise existing skills augmented with outside expertise.

Enlisting both business and IT teams into the project will help provide a balanced skill set to contextualise and analyse data while an outside expertise can fill the skills gap.

Too often, the conversation turns to the shortage of the elusive data scientists, when businesses can still succeed in delivering Big Data projects well by ensuring that the right team is pulled together from within the organisations existing skills sets.

Big Data, Data Ponds and Data Lakes: A Quick Reference Guide

Big Data has become a key driver in business project delivery, however do vast reservoirs of data translate into actionable engagement?

If you were to look at the business pages of almost any newspaper or attend a business conference, it's more than likely you'll come across the terms Big Data, Data Lake and now Data Pond.

Whether it's from the page, the lectern or the foyer, the subtext is that the conversation is all about data – and lots of it.

The primary business context for these terms relates to an organisation's ability to achieve the "ultimate 360 view" of the customer. Once gathered, the objective is to leverage this vast amount of information, or data, to provide the ultimate tailored customer experience.

It offers the potential to engage millions of people simultaneously, as well as targeting each individual in a bespoke manner.

The end game of gathering and organising these vast reservoirs of data is to use it to increased customer awareness and engagement on a level not possible before.

In order to achieve this level of performance and deliver that 360-customer view, new technologies and the corresponding buzzwords have emerged.

This is all great in theory but let's take a look at what Big Data, Data Lakes and Data Ponds really are. How do they differ from one another and why they are needed?

Here is the Quay Quick Reference Guide.

Definition: Big Data

Gartner defines Big Data as "high-volume, high-velocity and high-variety information assets that demand cost-effective, innovative forms of information processing for enhanced insight and decision making".

To the uninitiated this could be seen as the same purpose of the Data Warehouse (logical representation of clean, structured and vetted data).

The major differences include the sheer volume of data; the structured and unstructured nature of the data and the speed/velocity it is collected and utilised.

To give you an idea of the volume of data being collected:

- Facebook alone ingests 500 terabytes of new data every day
- Walmart handles 1 million transactions every hour and
- A Boeing 737 will generate 240 terabytes of flight data during a single flight.

The variety of data collected includes a mix of structured data with unstructured data such as photos, audio, videos, geospatial data and semi structured data such as unstructured text.

Definition: Data Lakes

Gartner refers to data lakes in broad terms as "enterprise wide data management platforms for analysing disparate sources of data in its native format".

The creation of data lakes has been the result of addressing the need for increased agility and accessibility for data analysis, since the traditional data warehouses have been found to be too rigidly structured to manage the volume, velocity and variety of data being collected.

Simply put instead of placing data in a purpose-built data store/data warehouse, you move it into a data lake in its original format where it is available to everyone. It also avoids the cost and time of transformation required with data warehouses but comes with some limitations due to the raw nature of how the data is now stored.

Thus the benefit of a Data Lakes in the short term is the upfront avoidance of costs and effort to understand, translate and categorise the data for structured relational storage (i.e.: The Data Warehouse model). The down side being the challenges around accessing the data due to it being kept in a rawer form.

Definition: Data Ponds

The responsibility of getting value out of the data reverts back to the business user and technologies such a Hadoop (a platform focused on the management of Big Data) are being used to assist in this.

However, without strong information governance, the risk is that the Data Lake will end up becoming a mismatch of unconnected collective reservoirs of data.

Thus we arrive at the third of our latest data terms the Data Pond also known as Data Puddles (in Australia we could also refer to them as Data Billabongs).

Deriving the value of Big Data

Turning Big Data into a usable and accurate source of information to get a 360-customer view has been a significant challenge.

However new tools and trends are emerging, such as Data Lakes and Hadoop which increasingly address organisation's data requirements.

Accurate reliable and reusable information with which to engage the end customer needs to become the norm.

Achieving this outcome still requires information governance; a clear vision of the outcomes and the right guidance and implementation to ensure success but this cannot be achieved without also embracing the latest data trends and buzzwords.

Next month we will look at why once captured Big Data and information management has been - and still is - such a challenge for organisations.

Big Data: A game changer we need to get right

Despite being touted as a significant technology trend, 'Big Data' has proven to be difficult to implement. How can business get it right?

Since 2008, more than $31 billion has been spent on Big Data projects, a figure expected to reach $114 billion by 2018.

The majority of business executives understand that Big Data is a serious technology disruptor, yet few have achieved success with their initiatives, according to a survey by Cap Gemini.

The survey found that only a quarter of the businesses surveyed classified their initiatives as successful, be they proof of concept, partially implemented or fully operational.

One could argue that the investment has led to unsuccessful outcomes, but given its potential as a game changer for the future of business, what are these businesses getting wrong and what measures can be put in place to set up Big Data projects for success?

Why are Big Data projects so challenging?

According to the study, the key challenges to getting these projects right included:

- Scattered data in silos across different teams
- Absence of a clear business case for funding and implementing Big Data projects
- Ineffective co-ordination of Big Data and analytics projects teams across the organisation
- Dependency on legacy systems for data processing and management
- Ineffectual governance models for Big Data and Analytics
- A lack of top management sponsorship
- Lack of clarity on Big Data tool and technology requirements

- The cost for tools and infrastructure
- Data security and privacy concerns
- Internal resistance to change within the organisation.

The survey flagged key technology challenges and in various degrees, vendors, technologists and Big Data Specialists have begun to address these challenges.

However, what this list also reveals is the importance of guiding principles behind successful project delivery, which are:

- Having a clear business case for any project
- Ensuring that there is effective coordination between project teams
- Implementing good governance
- Engaging the right sponsors
- Clarity around which tools should be used
- Bringing the team along on the journey

Defining what success looks like then qualifying it and putting in place the fundamentals of project management is essential for successful project delivery.

Without it, the old adage rings true: "Failing to plan means planning to fail" and that's where many Big Data projects become unstuck, as we explore below.

The business case

More than two thirds of businesses starting on their Big Data journey do not have well-defined criteria with which to measure the success of their initiatives, a critical activity for providing clear project goals and benchmarks for success.

Without a strong business case, starting on a project is like a ship starting off its journey without a destination, map or compass and still expecting to arrive.

Ensuring the business case is clear enables the executive and sponsors to understand the investment they signed off has not been wasted and the project has actually achieved something of importance for the business.

Tip: Have a clearly defined business case that identifies the problem, how it will be solved and what the benefit/s will be. Tailor it for the audience, i.e. CFO may be interested in the ROI, whereas the CMO may be more interested in the impact on Marketing.

Effective coordination and engagement between teams

Big Data projects impact a business across many teams, for example, IT, procurement, marketing, finance, sales and so on. Given that most Big Data initiatives require significant investment, these teams should be engaged throughout the lifecycle of the Big Data project.

Strong executive sponsorship is critical to success to ensure the project follows a top-down approach to drive this collaboration among teams. Without it, a Big Data initiative could result in lots of potentially aimless, unconnected activities being executed within the business under a the banner of a Big Data project.

Tip: Appoint a strong sponsor and support them with strategically placed champions (leaders) across the organisation.

Implementing good governance

There are three elements that will help deliver success if put in place appropriately: project governance, data governance and data ownership. These are critical because they ensure that the right information is provided to the right people at the right time throughout a project's delivery.

Tip: Review your data governance structure and identify the opportunities for improvement. Involve stakeholders across the organisations and establish buy in, KPIs and metrics that will ensure success.

Engaging the right influencers to bring users along for the journey

As Big Data projects impact on multiple parts of the organisation, aligning the stakeholders with a unified vision and engendering strong buy-in is critical to success. A short iterative "fail fast" approach delivers proof of concepts and quick wins, which will enable the project to demonstrate tangible value which can then be communicated to the wider business to build credibility and momentum. Clear consistent and tailored messaging, combined with strategic change leadership from the Big Data champions is a formula for success.

Tip: Always be generous in the amount to invest in change and communication management. It is the soft factor that contributes greatly to success. This team provides clarity, can break up the pockets of change resistance and ensures that messaging is strong and consistent.

Get the fundamentals right from the beginning

Big Data is becoming a critical tool for businesses and the ability to build a top down strategy and successfully deliver to the strategy will provide a significant competitive advantage. Other tips for Big Data projects include:

- Establish a well-defined organisational unit for Big Data initiatives that is closely integrated with business teams, to deliver a local business view of insights
- Create a senior leadership role for Big Data and analytics to signal the shift to a data-driven culture
- Establish clear criteria and metrics to measure the success of initiatives

Using good project delivery practices as outlined above complemented with the right technology will take you a long way towards success with your Big Data projects.

The Rise of Data Analytics: Where to in 2016?

As Big Data technology begins to mature, what is influencing the adoption of data analytics?

Big Data and focused Data Analytics are, without question, helping organisations make better decisions that are more informed; more profitable and more predictive.

In the current environment, businesses are increasingly driven to have a digital presence to prosper.

But more data isn't better data unless you know what to do with it. With access to big data starting to mature, analysing the right data is critical.

Whether you are selling products, attracting new prospects for the sales pipeline or creating brand awareness, information is the essential tool sitting behind your digital presence. Throw in the internet of things (IoT) and the data your phone, car, refrigerator, TV or fit bit yields, the volume starts to add up.

Post big data gold rush, where are we?

The so-called big data 'gold rush' has led organisations to invest in technology infrastructure, however many then struggle with the right skill base to derive value from the massive data lakes that accumulate.

If 2015 was all about the ability to capture and process data, 2016 will see many businesses looking to new technology to assist with the data analytics.

Machine learning, deep insights and predictive analytics are coming (if not already here), yet according to a recent IDG Enterprise report many still businesses remain behind the curve with less than forty percent of those surveyed would be investing in big data analytics in the short term.

Recent Australian technology recruitment data suggests otherwise, with an eight percent year-on-year rise for such roles relating to digital transformation projects, indicating that organisations need the human component of thinking, learning and interpreting that is sometimes overlooked in Big Data strategy.

Real-time analytics

Hadoop has given businesses significant access to the types of insights that big data can deliver and has given those businesses that invested early some advantage over those who come late to the party.

For many CIOs, however, it's not yet delivering the anticipated value. Business is shifting its focus from capturing and managing data to actively using it, meaning that the ability to measure data agility is becoming more important as is the shift to processing the data within data lakes.

The proliferation of devices and data sources has exploded the volume of data so that organisations are seeking better ways to pull actionable insights from data in real time and at speed to facilitate their use.

Some of the methods include pre-processing, filtering, aggregation and enriching data as it is captured, which enables more effective and more valuable querying of data lakes later.

There are significant benefits to investing in these methods as part of data capture and processing, namely that it enables faster access to insights that might linger or be lost inside traditional big data analytics. Data analytics – or data science – has a big role to play in enabling businesses to do that.

What are we measuring?

With the volume of data available, it is easy to get lost and not have clarity on the key measures required to make decisions. Aligning data analysis with what business objectives and outcomes are and working out how to measure those outcomes (the analysis) is the first critical step.

There isn't a one size fits all approach to suit all businesses. Here are some examples of the possible business objectives from the online world as a guide:

- **Ecommerce sites** – How many products or services are selling? How effectively are we servicing our customer's needs? Are we effectively marketing, remarketing and supporting the customer journey?
- **Lead generation sites** – Are we engaging and converting potential lead opportunities?
- **Content publishing sites** – What are our users interested in, engaging with and sharing?
- **Information or support sites** – How easy is it for users to find, access and engage with information as and when they need it?

These are measures of users behaviour within a digital marketing context, however by example, these questions align with greater business goals.

Measuring when, where, how and how often highlights if objectives are being achieved or the gaps where they are not.

It's not just an IT function

Marketers in retail, utility companies and telecommunications – to name a few – are increasingly looking for the technical skills required for data analytics and more of the talent is being recruited to sit in business units other than IT.

A recent report revealed that nine out of ten marketers are buying software such as web analytics and CRMs from within their own budgets, not from the IT budget.

36% of those purchases are for big data analytics tools to facilitate customer transaction analysis.

Half of those surveyed also suggested they are buying services or technology directly because they want flexibility and have a better understanding of what they need in the context of measuring consumer and business behaviour.

Organisations accumulate large volumes of data from many sources, much of it lacking structure as it is collect in databases, from websites, email, transactional software, devices and other sources.

Most of this information is being captured for customer services, marketing, sales and support reasons and the case for the 'single view' is challenging organisations to derive meaningful measurement and enable real-time decision-making.

As mentioned above, Australian businesses are already looking for the talent they need to implement data analytics projects to achieve exactly that.

One of the key challenges is finding the right skill sets to interpret, evaluate and utilise the insights gained from big data.

As the pace of data generation continues to accelerate, it's clear that data analysis strategy should factor into the business case of big data and be a key part of the management toolkit, not to mention this year's change and project budgets.

Big data is here to stay

The insights and information available from Big Data, if correctly aligned with business objectives and outcomes, can be transformational.

Knowing what and how to measure is critical to maximise the benefits. However, project fundamentals remain and planning and setting up a focused program/project with clear ownership and outcomes is vital to ensuring you are successful.

As your business on-boards the skills it needs, having the right project sponsors in place alongside good governance can make a considerable difference to outcomes.

CHAPTER 9

WHY GOVERNANCE IS ALWAYS THE KEY

The Key Considerations for Successful Project Governance

If project governance is not a 'one-size-fits-all' requirement for project success, how can organisations ensure they have the right type and amount of governance?

Good project governance is a critical factor for successful project delivery, however, what constitutes the 'right' type or amount of governance is often overlooked.

Many organisations stick to rigid models of project governance, irrespective of the type, size and risk profile of a project.

The problem with this approach is project governance is not a one-size-fits-all consideration and often issues arise with projects being either over or under-governed.

Either of these circumstances can adversely impact the successful outcome of projects. So what are some of the steps to consider when establishing a successful governance model for a project or program of work?

Understand the project risk profile

Risk is often the key factor for determining the amount of governance a project requires.

Risk comes in many forms. Projects could have a high-risk profile due to:

- large cost;
- complexity;
- the amount of transformation and change they are driving into a business or the potential risk to reputation if the project is unsuccessful;
- or a combination of all of the above.

During project initiation, this risk profile should be understood by the sponsor and project manager and factored into the project governance that is established.

Clear terms of reference

Often project governance can seem like just going through the motions.

Whilst the terms of reference of a governance committee and the accompanying roles and responsibilities may state otherwise, the general criticism from both sides of the table is an over-emphasis on reporting or providing general updates as opposed to genuinely 'governing' the project.

Project reporting is important in governance, meetings also need to focus on decision making and escalation forums should enable the project to be successful.

Ensure the terms of reference are correctly established to reflect this then ensure the members of the governance committee adhere to them.

Are the right people in the room?

We hear this time again and irrespective of the subject matter, governance is only as good as the people executing the terms of reference.

Make sure the members of the governance committee have the right job titles and/or delegated authority and ensure that they are willing to exhibit and model the correct behaviours.

A good starting point is to dedicate the first governance meeting to walking through the terms of reference of the committee and the roles and responsibilities of each member.

Don't assume everyone in the room knows why they are there or what is expected of them.

...and do they have the bandwidth?

Senior managers only have a finite amount of time to discharge both their BAU and project responsibilities. The time constraints of senior managers is a significant hurdle that should be factored in when selecting the members of a governance committee.

Whilst someone may be the right person to be on a governance board from a job title perspective, if they do not have the bandwidth to devote to the role it may be a better option to find someone else.

Persistent non-attendance or lack of engagement from a committee member should give pause for thought to potentially replacing this person.

Be prepared to manage up

A good project manager will know when the governance of their project is sub-optimal. They can either accept this fact and the issues it will cause their project or they can manage up and try and get the project governance the project requires.

Be confident to manage up in this situation. Raise the concerns with the sponsor and or directly with the committee itself.

The first casualty of poor project governance will not be the committee but more likely the project manager!

Fit-for-purpose governance

Very few projects can be successful without sound project governance. Whilst the points in this article are not exhaustive, they do provide a good checklist of what to look for when establishing fit for purpose project governance for a project.

Project governance is a nuanced beast and rarely a one-size fits all process. Take the time to ensure the governance for your project is sufficient and if it is not be willing to call out when the governance may be failing the project.

The governance committee will thank you in the end.

Setting up for success: The true value of reviews in project management

There is increasing recognition that assurance, undertaken by an independent party, is essential to project success.

Aside from the impartiality of an external project perspective, assurance provides a structured framework for ensuring that projects are routinely reviewed to stay on track, in scope and on budget.

So how do you ensure best bang for your assurance buck?

Health checks and post-implementation reviews

Two of the most common assurance mechanisms are health checks and post-implementation reviews (PIRs). Health checks help project teams to identify and correct problems before its too late, and are undertaken throughout the life of a project.

Post Implementation Reviews (PIRs) are a great way to capture project learnings gained during execution, which can subsequently be made available for other project teams.

Knowing where projects get off track

Recent Department of Defense analysis of more than 800 projects concluded that projects that were off-track and more than 15% into the execution invariably would not get back on-track.

The graphic below illustrates why. Note the position of typical health checks and where the PIR occurs – it's easy to see how a project can progress past the 15% mark before issues are addressed.

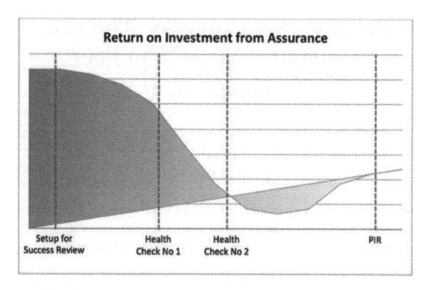

Return on Investment from Assurance

Setup for Success Review   Health Check No 1   Health Check No 2   PIR

Projects are typically front-loaded with activity and can get off-track very quickly. A Set up for Success Review held very early in the project development cycle will remediate any early problems.

The earlier the intervention, the less effort is required to change direction and lower the cost of the remediation.

Additionally, there is usually far less emotional energy invested by the project team, making it more likely they will be open and supportive of any required changes.

Setting up for success

Quay Consulting's Setup for Success Review approach combines both the P3M3 best practice key enablers for success together with the PMBOK 9 knowledge areas.

It delivers a comprehensive report that identifies the current state of critical success factors (CSFs) and makes recommendations where remediation is required.

An Executive Dashboard is presented in the format below with Red, Amber and Green traffic lighting representing the extent to which each component is configured for success. Health checks and PIRs have their place and are rightfully valued by business.

But Setup for Success Reviews are even more valuable because they occur well before the 15% mark that can derail a project.

Area Assessed	Status	Observation Summary
Management Control	◯	are there clearly defined outputs and outcomes, application of PMBOK knowledge areas and that governance is fit for purpose
Benefits Management	◯	ensuring there is clarity of definition, management and realisation plans in plan for project benefits
Financial Management	◯	appropriate involvement from the finance team, business case elements are complete, financial management is appropriate
Stakeholder Engagement	◯	internal and external stakeholders are analysed and engaged, communications planning is appropriate
Risk Management	◯	breadth and depth and maintenance, includes both risks and opportunities and value based strategies linked to benefits
Organisational Governance	◯	alignment to strategic imperatives, structures and representation
Resource Management	◯	All resources not just human, procurement processes, evidence of capacity planning and prioritisation to enable effective resource management, impact of resources outside the project team

Prevent rather than cure

An ounce of prevention is far better – and typically less costly – than a corrective cure. A Setup for Success Review, conducted early in the project lifecycle is the most powerful action you can take to ensure project success.

The relative return on investment (ROI) of different types of assurance activity illustrates why early intervention is important.

What is the right amount of Project Governance?

Project Governance is unarguably critical for the successful delivery of any project and too little Governance is a major contributing factor to project failure.

A lack of suitable Project Governance is by any measure one of the main reasons projects fail.

But what about if there is too much Governance or the Governance is focused in the wrong areas? This will also have adverse impacts on a projects success.

Whilst they may not 'fail' in the classic sense of the word they will produce less than optimal results.

So how can you assess if the Governance for your project or program is fit-for-purpose? While not exhaustive, the checklist below should offer a sound starting point when assessing if the Governance for your project has the project set up for success.

Are we seeing too much of each other?

Frequency of governance forums is also very important. Project managers and sponsors need to be mindful of not only the finite amount of time members of governance forums have to devote to their role but also ensuring there is enough clear air between forums for the project to keep delivering. It requires balance.

Meeting too infrequently can lead to critical decisions being delayed. Equally meeting too regularly can leave the project team in a constant state of reporting and preparation for various forums that can impact the focus on project deliverables.

A couple of good approaches to get this balance right is to have flexibility in the frequency with forums scheduled more often during critical project junctures or have forums run for longer during these times.

What would happen if we turned it off?

Governance for governance-sake can strangle a project. The adverse impacts include longer timelines due to slower decision-making or project resources being made to focus in the wrong areas on non-critical activities.

If there is a Governance forum that is not offering any value to the project, try simply discontinuing the forum or moving to a needs only basis. If it is critical forum the project manager will soon know.

Are we focused on the right areas?

If you view Governance as a key enabler for successful project delivery it is probably a projects most precious resource. And much like all other project resources it is finite.

Particularly given those who participate in Project Governance forums always have day jobs so their time must be used wisely.

It is critical then that once Governance forums are established the project manager and sponsor work very hard to regularly re-calibrate these sessions as required to ensure the project is always getting the right type of Governance and steerage in the right areas.

It is detailed... therefore it is good.

Alas, not always. Too much reporting or excessive information being presented to Governance forums can be a bad thing. It comes about for a few reasons:

Project Managers who feel compelled to report everything in the minutiae

Members of Governance forums who feel they need everything at their fingertips to make decisions and push for more and more in the updates.

Whatever the reason drowning Governance forums with too much information stymies crisp decision making.

Impacts include critical issues being lost among the large volumes of information, members of the governance forums becoming disengaged as they cannot possibly absorb all the data and the effort to compile these complex packs diverts a projects team's attention from delivering the project. Try and keep the information flow simple and succinct wherever possible.

Recalibrating project governance to suit

Successful Project Governance is not a one size fits all or a set and forget once it is established. Project Managers and Sponsors should understand this and always be open to re-calibrating their Project Governance forums and approaches to suit the current status of their projects to ensure they have the right amount and type of Governance at all times.

Six steps to aligning portfolios of work to business strategy

How can IT ensure that their projects are properly understood and aligned within the overall business strategy?

As a strategic partner with a purpose of supporting business outcomes it is imperative that IT understands where the business is going and aligns its strategy and hence initiatives to support business outcomes.

Too often IT believes they are undertaking initiatives to benefit the business only to find the initiatives don't deliver or aren't aligned to the business strategy.

Some of the reasons this happens are:

- The business strategy hasn't been translated into IT usage and capabilities
- IT haven't understood the real business drivers
- The business has moved on - outcomes of initiative are no longer relevant
- The initiative was done in isolation within IT and imposed on the business without consultation and hence there is limited or no buy in from the business
- This leads to some fairly vital questions that IT need to resolve to ensure that their programs align tightly with business strategy, such as:
- How can IT ensure that they understand the business strategy?
- How can they develop a model and roadmap that enables all stakeholders (including the business) to easily understand – and agree – on projects that are aligned to the company strategy?

Architecture principals + capability modelling = alignment

Quay has found that one way of achieving both the understanding and the model and roadmap is to use Architecture principles combined with Capability Modelling to align business strategy and IT delivery.

Mapping out business operations as a functional view (i.e. the what, not the how), via capability modelling produces a clear one-page diagram of the business functions and how IT support each function through, applications, information, infrastructure and people.

Once produced this enables the business and IT to see where gaps and duplications exist when planning for the future and provides a roadmap for projects and portfolios of work.

CIOs can than have informed discussions with the business and IT teams alike using an easily understood model as the centre piece for decision making.

How it works

The diagram below illustrates how IT Architecture and IT Organisational Capability is influenced by the Business and conversely how it supports then business.

When these functions are is not aligned then business outcomes cannot be achieved. This knowledge combined with the six-step approach we have provided delivers a significant step towards alignment between the Company Strategy and IT.

Six Steps to Alignment

1. Develop and agree a 'current state' Business Capability Model

This ensures that the business strategy has been articulated to a level that is translatable to IT usage and capabilities of the business are agreed and understood by IT.

2. Develop a target state Application, Information & Infrastructure Architecture based on the business Capability Model

Takes a current and future snapshot of Technology and Organisation footprints and ensure the future state fully supports the business and IT strategy. Typically included in this is:

- Current State summary
- Future State Capability Model
- Target State Architecture across applications, information and infrastructure

3. Deliver a target IT Organisational Structure and functional role requirements

Outlines the most effective structure to support the business, considers strategies such as outsourcing, cloud etc.

Also what are the functions and roles needed to support the business and what are the gaps? Typically includes:

- Target IT Organisational Chart
- Functional Roles and responsibilities
- IT Organisational Capability Model
- Outline of Gaps

4. Create an IT Strategy that includes the target application, information & infrastructure architectures and organisational structure

An IT Strategy provides a coherent and holistic approach to supporting the business strategy for all IT investments and changes and typically includes:

- IT Strategy Principles
- Definitions of how IT will support the business
- How IT will support business agility
- Articulates how IT is aligned to the business
- Implication of the Business Strategy on IT
- Pain Points

5. Build a roadmap for change

Provides clearly articulated stages to get to the future state as a sequence of activities that will generate value to the businesses processes.

Typically includes:

- A dimensioned roadmap of projects to move to future state
- Reference Architecture
- Criteria for roadmap decisions
- Guiding principles

6. Plan out a program of works

Provides the guidance and governance for a portfolio of works that deliver the determined work packages aligned to the business strategy.

Typically includes:

- Portfolio of dimensioned projects
- Defined criteria against time, costs, complexity, business benefit etc.

Utilising the six-step approach, IT can ensure that they understand how their projects and programs will work within the context of the overall business strategy.

Secondly, they have the capacity to articulate, frame and build a roadmap that ensures that projects are aligned from the outset and remain aligned throughout the implementation phase.

When is it time to call in the project recovery team?

If you find yourself with a project that is underperforming or overrunning time and cost, it is possible to steer a project back on track if the right steps are taken.

If you find yourself with a project that is underperforming or overrunning time and cost, it is possible to steer a project back on track if the right steps are taken.

In 2011 Victoria's Ombudsman handed down one of the most damning assessments of public sector IT project governance in Australia's history, noting total cost over-runs of $1.44 billion, extensive delays and a general failure to actually deliver. The report highlighted the systemic failure to respond to critical measures indicating that the projects were not on track.

This is a very public example of an all too familiar litany of high profile project failures.

However, it serves to highlight the need to set projects up for success from the outset, or at the very least understand when it's time to bring in project recovery expertise.

If you find yourself with a project that is not performing, engaging a project recovery team early – before the horse has bolted – can ensure projects can be successfully delivered before cost and time overruns cause the promised outcomes to evaporate.

Aim to set up for success but know when you're in trouble

In 2012, we highlighted the value of Setting up for Success (Quay Bulletin #2), particularly the use of regular project reviews as a highly effective way to mitigate project failure.

Regular health checks can provide high value returns by evaluating the project's progress and where recommendations are made, by ensuring they are implemented properly. Too often findings from health checks are ignored or watered down during implementation.

However, depending on how far behind a project is or if overruns are emerging, a health check may not be enough of an intervention and corrective action must be taken.

So when is the right time to bite the bullet and call in a project recovery team?

Indicators you need project recovery support

Quay's consultants are regularly called into help get projects back on track and in our experience, there are some key indicators that should red flag the need for project recovery support.

Whilst not exhaustive, below is a list of circumstances that if present may indicate time to consider engaging a recovery project team:

- Two Health Checks performed and no improvement
- Lack of clearly defined benefits
- Organisation is not ready for the change (lack of Change Management)
- Poor Governance (roles and responsibilities and decision making process unclear)
- Repeatedly missed milestones and deliverables
- Constant ambiguity about the requirements
- Stakeholders are not engaged or communicated with
- Little to no evidence of risk management
- Out of date schedules that no longer support the project
- Budgets that continually overrun against deliverables

The good news is that the recovery process offers a high rate of success and can save businesses substantial time and money.

Project recovery

There are a number of fundamental guiding principles to follow to help ensure any project recovery exercise undertaken will be successful:

Don't reinvent the wheel – leverage the significant amount of work already done by previous health checks, reviews or project artefacts.

Create momentum - seek to deliver value quickly

Existing expertise - Use the expertise of the team to correctly assess and develop a fit-for-purpose, pragmatic recovery plan, rather than relying on standardised diagnostic tools and outputs.

Outcomes focused - Ensure all activities are directly related to the achievement of the success-based outcomes.

Success focused recovery

Asking "what does success look like for the project?" and "what corrective actions are required?" go a long way to jumpstarting the process.

Once the guiding principles are in place it is important that the recovery team follow the next steps to ensure the project recovery is a success.

1. Identify 'quick wins' and move to implement these

Early identification of benefits and delivering quick wins can change the energy of a project and its team from failures, exhaustion and disillusion to being re-energised with successes.

2. Project Governance – Sponsorship and Steering Committees

A review of the governance structure will quickly inform you if the project governance arrangements meet best practice, are fit for purpose and if the project is setup for success.

3. How ready is the business to embrace the change?

Assessing business change readiness will give the organisation great insight into the level of engagement with the business:

- Is the business ready to embrace the change?
- Do they know what success looks like? have they been consulted on their needs?
- And do they understand the immediate and long term impact and benefits?
- What change management strategies and plans are in place?

4. Project Artefacts

Start by reviewing the project artefacts including schedule, requirements, test planning, budget, health checks, resource plans, and risk and issues management.

This confirms the current state baseline of the project and the status or prior recommendations and agreed actions.

This is by no means an exhaustive list as there are a number of activities that must be undertaken to ensure project recovery is a success.

Getting back on track

What's important to note is that it is possible to steer a project back on track if the right steps are taken. The objective is to ensure that the project will deliver the benefits to the business as originally envisaged.

Bringing in outside expertise at the right time can be the difference between successfully turning a project around and a failing project.

CHAPTER 10

PROJECT MANAGEMENT: THE THINGS THEY DON'T TEACH YOU AT SCHOOL

How is a project defined?

A review of an organisation's project slate will reveal most in-flight projects meet the basic criteria of cost, risk and complexity to comfortably be deemed a project.

But like most things, it is the outliers that can create the greatest challenge, i.e. the initiatives on the margins that may or may not need project disciplines to be delivered successfully.

Whilst not exhaustive, we've outlined a list of the criteria that should be worked through to help develop a project classification framework to decide what constitutes a project for your organisation.

It might be small but is it risky?

The amount of risk an initiative will take on is a key determining factor as to whether it should be shaped up and run as a project or not.

Many projects fail due to poor risk management or the inability of those delivering the outcomes to identify and manage risk effectively. An initiative can be small in reach and budget but due to a high-risk profile may be deemed worthy of being run as a project.

The types of considerations to take into account during this assessment include:

- Whether the initiative is client facing and
- Are there other larger projects dependent upon its successful outcomes?
- What's the cost?

This is probably the easiest measure to both quantify and justify when classifying a project.

Organisations have a finite change budget and the more money they are investing in an initiative the higher the stakes and therefore closer the scrutiny.

Typically, organisations will set a threshold (say $50K – $100K+) and anything above this will be deemed a project.

Often to allow flexibility and nimbleness during execution organisations will have a sliding scale whereby the greater the costs of the project the more rigid the adherence to the mandated project delivery methodology and governance structures.

When assessing an initiative on the margin against the cost criteria organisations should be mindful of ensuring all potential project costs are captured including the effort of permanent staff and support costs and that the costs are not hidden to keep below a set threshold.

How complex is it?

Initiatives will often fail due to their complexity, particularly if the activities are across multiple areas of the business with multiple interdependencies.

The greater the complexity of an initiative the greater the need for sound project disciplines to help ensure project delivery.

Some techniques that can be used to help assess if a project needs to be established is to look at the solution architecture to assess how many systems or processes are impacted, or to review the stakeholder matrix to understand the broader business and organisational impacts that may warrant the establishment of a project.

Have we been here before?

When an organisation is doing something for the very first time the initiative will typically benefit from good project disciplines.

On the flip side there will be times when an organisation is repeatedly executing similar types of initiatives that due to the delivery becoming part of the organisations DNA they may not need to be run as full-scale projects.

This is a judgment call for the executive but familiarity can and will play a part in deciding when a project should be established.

Solid foundations and frameworks

Whilst the above list is not exhaustive, it should provide a sound foundation to establish a framework to assess projects against. Classifying projects is not an exact science and judgment and experience still need to play a part.

Establishing a solid framework to score initiatives against using some basic criteria is the first step in ensuring all projects that should be run as projects are run as projects.

Putting business back into business case

If your IT projects are IT centric, you may be ignoring the business partnership opportunities that IT has to offer.

Failing to factor business into the benefits of IT-driven initiatives risks IT being perceived as a service provider rather than a key enabler and business partner.

At a time when service providers are increasingly being outsourced, how can IT teams enable and partner with the business to deliver on the organisation's goals?

Understanding the 'business case'

The IT team needs to ensure that they have a strong business focus and contribute effectively to building the business case.

A 2008 study by *Peppard, Ward and Daniel* [ii]highlighted a common mistake in building the business case was only including the financial benefits and IT-focused efficiency improvements.

Building Better Business Cases for IT Investments also flagged a high correlation between project failure rates and the lack of business benefits included in the business case.

The same study identified that organisations that were more successful in realising value from their IT investments understood that the business case is not only a way of obtaining funding, but serves other purposes such as:

- Ensuring commitment from business managers to achieving the intended benefits
- Identifying how the combination of IT and business changes will deliver each of the benefits identified
- Enabling informed prioritised decision making on allocating funds and resources

- Creating a basis for reviewing whether the expected business benefits are actually realised
- Partnering with the business and focusing on projects that add value and are key business enablers ensure IT stays relevant and is valued by the business.

An example: Desktop Deployment

Desktop deployment offers a good illustration of how understanding the business case and engaging with the business is critical for success.

The yardstick measurement for ensuring a project stays on course and delivers the benefits to the business should include:

- Starting the business case for desktop deployment from within the business
- Ensuring that IT has engaged all parts of the business in their strategy planning
- Understanding the needs and benefits (both soft and hard)
- Definition of how IT will measure those benefits to the business

By way of example business benefits for desktop deployment projects could include:

- Application rationalisation
- Detailed knowledge of what applications, documents and devices are critical to the business
- New features and benefits the desktop can bring to the business
- Capability uplift and functional enhancements to current ways of working

By partnering with the business, IT teams can help management understand more effectively how each of these benefits will deliver effective, sustainable change for the business.

That partnership and the ability to put 'business' into the business case will ensure that IT is seen as a vital part of the team, not just as a service provider.

The pros and cons of outsourcing project delivery

When is it appropriate to consider outsourcing the delivery of your organisation's projects?

There are myriad of ways to successfully deliver projects and one of the critical considerations is whether to delivery all of your organisation's projects in-house or to selectively outsource some of them.

Whilst all organisations should strive to develop an in-house project delivery capability, there are some circumstances where outsourcing is the more appropriate option and can lead to better project outcomes.

However, it is vital that the decision to outsource a project is done for the right reasons. It's not a simple case of one is better than the other both approaches have their pros and cons.

Often the decision comes down to the nature of the project as much as an organisation's in-house capability. So, what are the key considerations that should be taken into account when deciding whether to outsource a project for delivery or to keep it in-house?

Do you have the in-house expertise?

Many organisations have projects that are 'one-offs' and require specialist expertise to deliver effectively. It is a significant investment to source and build an internal team with the requisite skills, a cost that may be far greater than by following an outsourcing strategy.

Whilst building in-house expertise should always be a consideration, in certain instances once the project is completed, the skills developed by the internal team may simply not be portable due to the one off nature of the project.

Engaging a partner with runs on the board in an area unfamiliar to the business will reduce the risk of delivery and – if managed well – will increase the opportunity for a quality outcome for the project.

Is it a repeatable project?

Paradoxically projects that are repeatable are often very good candidates for outsourcing.

With repeatable projects, vendors will have identified the regular needs within their client base, which allows them to develop strong capability and retain expertise.

A good example is desktop computer upgrades.

Upgrading your organisation's desktop computers is a regular occurrence and it may make more sense to identify a partner who does this type of project repeatedly and leverage their expertise and IP rather than mobilise an internal team every three years or so.

Will the outsource partner have skin in the game?

This is more a consideration once a decision has been made to outsource.

First and foremost, a delivery partner should be identified with the expertise that is required to execute the project.

The next step is to assess if your selected partner has sufficient skin in the game to ensure they will be full committed to the right outcomes for the duration of the project.

Whilst contractually there are some safe guards that can be put in place in terms of SLAs and similar agreements, this should not replace due diligence and significant efforts on the part of both parties to foster an extremely collaborative relationship for the duration of the project.

This is best achieved if the relationship is established from the outset to be less master/servant and more one of a partnership.

What is the risk to the business if the project fails?

All projects have a certain risk profile that will impact the business if they fail. It is important to fully appreciate this risk to the business of failure when deciding the best delivery approach.

Outsourcing can appear the costlier option at the outset but this should be set against the potential cost, operational and reputational impact to the business of project failure.

Typically, the greater the potential adverse impact to the business of project failure then the more consideration should be given to different delivery approaches including outsourcing the project to a specialist partner.

Due diligence, contextual assessment & governance

The above list is not exhaustive nor can it hope to cover all the various individual considerations organisations need to take into account when deciding how to best deliver a slate of projects.

However, outsourcing is a proven delivery model and should be given due consideration when an organisation is deciding how best to deliver a diverse portfolio of projects.

Regardless of the delivery approach taken, outsourced projects should still be covered by sound portfolio management and internal project governance if the best results are to be achieved.

Resetting a failing project for successful delivery

How can a business re-set a project to bring it back into alignment with strategy?

It's a pretty rare phenomenon that a project progresses from inception through to implementation without encountering issues along the way.

However there are some red flags that signal a project is more than just encountering its share of challenges but that in fact it is starting to fail.

Chronic cost over-runs, continual scope creep, repeated missed delivery milestones, poor project moral and project misalignment are just some of the indicators that a project is on the road to failing to deliver any of its originally stated benefits.

Projects typically show signs of failing when governance isn't robust enough or when a project has a protracted rollout – it's not uncommon for long-term projects to lose sight of the requirement to align to business strategy or for your teams to experience project fatigue.

For a project to fall into the 'fail' category, however, the issues confronting the project are significant and require special attention to get them back on track.

While it may be that shutting down a project is the most obvious course of action, it is a difficult process and may not be the right decision.

An alternative? Resetting the project to ensure success. Let's explore some of the areas that should demand attention when turning a project around.

Review and redefine the governance

A failing project will invariably have issues within the existing governance structure. The project cannot proceed to a successful outcome unless these issues are addressed and a fit for purpose governance structure is put in place.

But to achieve that, there is often need for a frank and open discussion at the right level, be it the steering committee or at the project board, to identify the issues and fix them. This can mean radical surgery such as:

- Replacing sponsors or project managers
- Scrapping existing steering committees
- Re-establishing governance forums at a more senior level
- Redefining the terms of reference.

Either way the project manager should not proceed with the project until they are comfortable the right governance is in place with suitably experienced and committed personnel who have the bandwidth to execute their roles.

In our experience, this type of "project surgery" benefits from the outside perspective of independent facilitators who are able to help identify fundamental issues within a project without bias or blame.

Re-connect with the team

There is a high probability the team working on a failing project will be suffering significant project fatigue, quite possibly be disengaged and jaded due to their 'brand' being linked to a failing project, which is often very public.

Re-energising a team and convincing them that the project re-set is going to work is vital to turning it around. The project manager and sponsor should ensure they:

- Initiate one-on-one discussion with key team members
- Explain clearly the new approach and actively solicit feedback where appropriate
- Implement value-add suggestions.

It may also require some team members being moved off the project if they cannot get out of a negative mindset or they lack the required skill set for the future.

It is also a good idea to stage a kick-off event to signify that the project is under new command and is now set to deliver.

Address the top issues

While it may sound simplistic, no project reset has a chance of success if the main showstoppers have not been identified and adequately addressed.

There is a reason that a project is failing and until the issues are identified, acknowledged and remediated, the project simply cannot be set upon a successful path.

To help facilitate this, a project re-set should be accompanied by an independent project review to flesh out all issues, have them ranked in order of importance and impacts and have them addressed accordingly.

Simply replacing the project manager for example (which is a typical knee jerk reaction) will not turn the project around if there are underlying issues that are not being acknowledged and resolved.

Have patience

This is a special plea to senior management. Project delivery is difficult at the best of times, let alone when a project has gone off the rails. Patience and suitable support from the executive go a long way to ensuring that new plans being put into place can be realised.

This will give the new governance and project team the time to address issues, re-set the team and set the project back on the right track. It will not happen overnight but it may not happen at all if the team is not given some additional breathing space.

Projects can and will fail. But they can be saved and turned around to achieve successful outcomes with the right attention to a few key areas.

The above list is not exhaustive but is hopefully a good starting point if your organisation is embarking on the journey to turn around a failing project.

Large-scale ERP: A thing of the past?

ERPs have been a mainstay in large-scale project delivery. As Agile and innovation projects become more prominent, is it time to consign ERPs to the past?

Enterprise resource planning – or ERP – has been a longstanding trend for large-scale project delivery. Yet while the term "ERP" has become part of the modern business lexicon and can deliver significant organisational benefits, it would appear that the trend is shifting away from ERP implementation.

Many organisations are instead adopting agile or online self-service systems and technical innovation is driving alternative methods for project delivery.

So is ERP in steep decline and how will that impact the types of projects selected for delivery?

What is an ERP?

ERP stands for Enterprise Resource Planning and is typically a stand-alone suite of integrated business applications that services the entire company's business processes.

The aim of the ERP system is to break down the silos within a business and thereby gain benefits from the integration of all core business processes across the organisation, including:

- Process improvements
- Cost reductions
- Synergies from sharing information

ERP implementations are large scale project undertakings and impact the entire business, thus the cost of implementation is a significant investment for any organisation.

What does a "typical ERP" look like?

Typically, ERP systems rely upon big data stored and controlled centrally. Successful implementations require long project lead times to gather requirements, design and implement if done properly.

Furthermore, the ERP market is dominated by very large software vendors who follow well planned project delivery methodologies to ensure ERP implementations are successful but this too comes with a hefty price tag.

Why are ERP implementations declining?

Whilst ERP solutions can offer undoubted benefits for an organisation the current trend is to move away from ERPs. Some of the new business thinking driving this shift away from ERP implementations includes:

It's got to be Agile to get the benefits

Undoubtedly the biggest shift in project delivery thinking and practice over the last five years is moving more toward an "Agile way of doing things".

Agile project delivery, unlike waterfall, is not big bang but seeks to deliver project outcomes, and more importantly the benefits, incrementally.

Most organisations are adopting Agile techniques for projects where it is appropriate ie: software development projects with significant opportunities for business process re-engineering.

An Agile approach ensures benefits are delivered regularly and learnings are carried forward to the next cycle or sprint.

ERP implementation by their very nature do not lend themselves to Agile techniques. They are delivered by Waterfall methodologies and require long lead times. More importantly they require an executive to sign off on a business case that will not deliver benefits until sometimes far off into the future which senior executives are increasingly reluctant to do instead preferring regular and consistent delivery of benefits.

On-line self service systems

The pendulum that once drove the large uptake of ERP systems i.e. the desire to break down the silos within an organisation, is now swinging back in the other direction.

The proliferation of on-line self-service systems is creating a new way of doing business where data and processes are segmented off by an organisation and accessed on-line by users thus re-creating the silos's ERP systems sought to break down.

Innovation is the way forward

All organisations need to innovate to ensure they can remain relevant and successful in their market space. This is particularly true with the pace of change occurring in most sectors.

Innovation by its very nature needs to happen quickly to keep pace with the speed of change and should work on the principle of "fail fast".

This is giving rise to project innovation funds whereby small teams are afforded the freedom to pursue business objectives sometimes outside the normal project delivery structures.

Often known as Skunkworks, this trend is moving away from the large scale, time consuming and expensive ERP solutions of the past to a leaner and more nimble approach to delivering change in an organisation.

Big data can now be in the Cloud

One of key drivers of a successful ERP is big data. The capture, storage and access of the company data across all divisions was greatly enhanced by ERP solutions.

With the increasing use of the Cloud for an organisation's data needs, the case for an ERP is no longer as compelling, particularly when you look at the cost savings the user pay model the public Cloud can offer.

Whilst the large scale ERP solution is not dead, it is certainly on the decline and this is impacting on the types of projects that are now receiving funding approval for delivery.

The current generation of project managers will need to be mindful of this trend and be adaptable to the new project delivery landscape.

Skeleton Teams: Making the Impossible Possible

Few projects end with the team they started with and are often under resourced. So can a skeleton team deliver more with less?

Very few projects end with the team they originally commenced with or thought they would need.

The resource requirements for a project are often understated during project establishment due to a variety of factors, for example, overly optimistic estimates to keep costs under control or incorrect assumptions about skills required through every phase of delivery.

Priorities also change and what were once ring-fenced resources can be pulled away from your project and redirected to work on new business priorities. Requests for additional resources will often fall on deaf ears due to lack of funds or the organisation may not have spare capacity or the right people.

So if more resources aren't the answer, is it possible to deliver more with less? The short answer is yes and we outline below some techniques that will help deliver projects successfully that are under-resourced.

The Planning

If a project is under-resourced it is imperative there is no wastage in the allocation of resources to the planned tasks. Planning in this instance is critical.

If the planning is executed to a high degree of quality, it will protect against wastage during execution and help ensure the limited resources are always where they can add the most value to the project outcomes.

Project Managers need to take the time up front to drive quality into their project plans and identify any unnecessary or over allocated tasks and remove or adjust them in the schedule as required.

Scope

The Project Manager with a skeleton team cannot allow for scope creep. The more scope added to a project, the more pressure will be exerted on an already under-resourced team.

It is imperative that the Project Manager keep well on top of the scope of the project and negotiate change requests for any additional scope so they will receive additional funds, resources etc. to cater for the additional tasks.

Governance and Stakeholder Management

Stakeholder management and communication can often suffer in under-resourced teams.

The Project Manager can be more focused on helping deliver the solution to cover for lack of resources, this can be detrimental to their stakeholder management responsibilities.

Instead, the Project Manager should focus their energy on:

- Aligning the project with business strategy;
- Understanding each stakeholder (Internal & External) and their drivers; and
- Communicating clearly and regularly.

Achieving genuine alignment between the business and IT solution is a significant step towards success, particularly when it is supported by a governance structure containing strong sponsorship and stakeholders who clearly understand their remit.

It is a critical requirement that there are clear channels of communication (both formal and informal) to enable the Project Manager to keep key stakeholders regularly informed of challenges the project is facing, in particular any resource constraints. The "no surprises" principle is critical here – key players must be aware of the challenges within the project.

Pick the A Team

Selecting the project team, especially one that is under-resourced, means that the level of talent procured is crucial. High performing experts who are in critical roles for the project's duration can significantly lift the performance and productivity of all individuals within the team. It's a clear case of quality over quantity.

A study by McKinsey & Co underscores the importance of these two points when looking at the biggest cause of project failures. The report found that 50% of all cost overruns result from a lack of focus on stakeholders and talent within the team.

Short outcome led cycles

Agile projects specialise in leveraging small teams to deliver high levels of output. Utilising some of the principles of Agile and running short packages of work with quantifiable outcomes can help create a sense of real progress and success.

This can be vital to the success of an under-resourced team that may be working long hours to help keep them energised and focused.

Decision-making

A small experienced team can deliver significant amounts in short cycles if supported by the right decision-making framework that allows for quick turn arounds of decisions required.

Slow or poor decision-making frameworks will eat into valuable time that an under resourced team simply does not have.

It is therefore critical to project success to ensure the decision-making framework is both robust and nimble to allow for crisp decision making when required.

Quality over quantity is most valuable

Quay has found that, more than anything, sound project delivery comes down to the quality of the team not necessarily the quantity of the people on the team.

A skinny team with the right people and supported by good planning, scope control and robust stakeholder management has a high chance of success.

We believe experienced professionals working together within a unified and well-governed project can achieve significant results even when short-staffed.

Whilst the above list is not exhaustive it is a good starting point in how to deliver a project successfully with less rather than more.

The Case for the Honest Project Delivery Broker

All too often a project fails because of a breakdown in the relationship between customer and vendor. Enter the case for an independent 'broker' to keep everyone honest.

It's an all-too-common situation: when we look at projects that are in trouble, very often the culprit is a breakdown in the relationship between a customer and a vendor. Eyes have been taken off the delivery of the scope and vital energies have been diverted from the project to dealing with conflict management.

This breakdown can lead to a damaging blame culture and ultimately threats of commercial penalties from both sides. Given the prevalence of this at times toxic vendor-customer dynamic in a failing project, we've identified the systemic issues that often arise and how to avoid it happening to both your current and future projects.

The key takeout? Our review shows that having an independent partner with a mandate for keeping all parties honest generally leads to better outcomes.

So what do you need to be aware of at the beginning of a vendor relationship and how can the engagement of an 'honest Project Delivery broker' help turn your projects around?

Governance – Avoid creating an "Us-and-Them culture"

Promoting an open, transparent conversation between the customer and the vendor can go a long way to avoiding a breakdown in a project's delivery.

In a number of instances, we found that whilst a critical stakeholder in the delivery of the project, vendors are frequently left off the overarching steering body (e.g. Project Steering Committee). Internal

Project Managers typically provide updates, which can present a siloed view of progress, risks and issues.

Where a vendor's performance has been questioned, there is often no open forum to present their case or work collaboratively to create "one team", which can lead to an "us-and-them" culture – the first step on the path to failure.

Of course there are instances when it isn't appropriate to include vendors in the reporting process, particularly where there are commercial sensitivities involved.

Quay takeaway: The engagement of an honest broker promotes open and transparent discussions across the key stakeholders to drive effective governance by a unified team.

Project Management Plan – Create and Manage to a single integrated plan

A Project Management Plan is essential to avoiding a disconnect – and often misalignment – between the various resources delivering a project. The Project Management Plan should clearly describe:

- The end-to-end schedule
- A complete Work Breakdown Structure
- How the project will be managed (e.g. PMBOK: time, cost, resources, procurement, integration risk, stakeholders etc.)

The disconnect often becomes a divide when a vendor is seen to be project managing, as they are naturally focused on delivery their component of the solution (e.g. software implementation, configuration and so on) whilst in many cases, no one is managing change, benefits or enterprise architecture.

Quay takeaway: The honest broker manages the project as a single team delivering the entire scope of the project, irrespective of who the resources work for.

Business Case – Ensure the validity of "the Case for Change"

Most projects start their life with a business case that justifies the reasons a project should be undertaken, including the context for the project, its scope and the outcomes it will deliver.

If a vendor is managing its delivery, the vendor's focus naturally is on delivering their components, not the business benefits and the case for change. The problems arise when there is no clear link back to decisions made as to whether the project should proceed, if scope is changed or the benefits are revisited.

Quay takeaway: The honest broker holds the validity of the Case for Change as their number one priority. If the project is at risk of not being delivered on its promise, they call it out early.

Change – "a solution without change management is a recipe for failure"

A vendor can deliver the most eloquent technical solution in the world, but without managing the change impacts within the business, the solution's success is at risk.

Successful technical deployment does not necessarily guarantee translation to a "successful project".

Change management activities must be owned by the business as part of an overall integrated plan. It is not enough to have the business manage change and the vendor manage the solution: there must be an overarching plan with linked milestones and dependencies.

Quay takeaway: The honest broker understands the technical project management aspects as well as the human change elements in a project, then ensures all are proactively managed and appropriately linked as part of a single delivery.

Successful projects don't happen by luck

Successful projects don't happen by 'luck' and the old adage rings true: relationships are built not bought.

Engaging an 'honest broker' to manage the project means a business is far more likely to avoid a damaging relationship breakdown than if your solution is managed exclusively by the vendor or even your own internal project managers.

The independence of the honest broker means they remain focused on the promise of the case for change, view the project holistically and build a strong single, integrated team from the top down regardless of who the project actors work for.

Their responsibility is to ensure these elements rally around the benefits of the business case, whilst also holding the client and the vendor to account. This is vital in eliminating the likelihood of an 'us-and-them' culture and ultimately the client-vendor blame game.

Vendor-led projects: A fox in the hen house?

Is allowing a vendor to lead the project management of solution implementation the equivalent to letting the fox run the hen house?

There is little doubt that implementing new technology or solutions into a business can be a difficult task and all too often, it's the dynamic between the customer and the vendor that is the crux of most of the challenges.

Embarking on the customer-vendor journey is a long-term relationship that requires significant trust on both sides.

This critical relationship tends to run into trouble from the outset when vendors become responsible for project delivery beyond their technical piece, particularly when there are differing points of view on what is being delivered.

Once issues begin to arise both vendor and customer's eyes can be taken off the delivery of the scope, which can lead to vital energies being diverted from the project to dealing with conflict management.

Typically engaging an independent integrator to execute the project from the outset can considerably reduce the risk of a toxic environment forming between the vendor and client and lead to better project outcomes.

Either way these projects are always a challenge and we explore below some of the fundamental reasons why getting vendors to deliver your projects may not always be the right approach.

Different definitions of what success looks like

The reality is that the vendor and client organisation will approach a project from two different perspectives, neither of which should be ignored. While both share the common goal of getting the product implemented, the desired outcomes and definition of success may differ.

The vendor is interested in seeing its product implemented; its team is focused on the content of the effort, which involves the actual execution of the technology. The organisation's perspective reaches far beyond that goal, focusing on the outcomes resulting from the project, or the context perspective.

The organisation needs to take a broader view of the implementation process and manage the risks, benefits and changes the organisation will experience throughout the process to include the actual implementation as well as parallel activities affected by the implementation, such as the change management and on-going use and support of the system.

These differing perspectives affect the expectations, goals and approach taken by each party during the engagement.

For example, the vendor is typically focused on reaching a "go-live" date in the shortest time frame possible, as its contractual agreements usually structure the largest payment to occur at that time, which can lead to Vendor project managers not being focussed on Business Case benefits.

Understanding the business case

Most projects start their life with a business case that justifies the reasons a project should be undertaken, including the context for the project, its scope and the outcomes it will deliver. If a vendor is managing its delivery, the vendor's focus naturally is on delivering their components not the business benefits and the case for change.

Due to this potential narrow focus, problems arise when there is no clear link back to decisions made as to whether the project should proceed, if scope is changed, or the benefits are revisited. These are all issues that lead to poorly integrated project plans.

The disconnect between delivering the solution but not the project

Project managers should be responsible for delivery of the fully integrated project plan including the end-to-end schedule and a detailed Work Breakdown Structure for all key activities and deliverables.

There is often a disconnect when a vendor is project managing, as they are naturally focused on delivery of their component of the solution (e.g. software implementation, configuration and so on) to the exclusion or detriment of all other activities.

This can lead to no one in the project effectively managing key deliverables like change, benefits realisation or the creation of a sustainable enterprise architecture for the system.

Is the fox looking after the hen house?

Are vendors measured on product sold, additional consulting services rendered (including building future complexity into solutions) or successful implementations?

A recent study of a failed vendor led project in the USA (implementation of Patient Management system into a small hospital) elicited this observation from the client's lawyer, that the vendor, instead of providing "one throat to choke," provided "many products to buy".

After the initial engagement was signed, the focus of the large vendor moved to expanding their offerings and re-interpreting the scope of the project.

Quay observed similar issues on a recent Australian client site whereby the vendor responsible for the configuration and customisation work was also responsible for the project delivery.

This is essentially the fox looking after the hen house.

The situation led to significant scope creep and the implementation of an overly cumbersome, heavily customised solution that did not achieve the business case benefits. The project did not get back on track until the vendor project manager layer was replaced with independent project management.

Can the vendor deliver the end-to-end solution?

Successful project delivery requires skills beyond simply managing in-house technical teams which is typically a vendor supplied project manager's strength.

There will be many stakeholders, teams and individuals that need to be managed beyond the Vendor's technical resources.

The critical question is this: Does the Vendor have the requisite skilled personnel to deliver the end to end solution?

Due to their narrow focus, Vendors may not possess project resources that have the ability to manage beyond the technical for a project which can create a skills gap and adversely impact the delivery of the entire project scope and if they do, will the Vendor assign their "A" team to the delivery?

Whether your project is assigned the best project delivery resources depends on the vendors other competing priorities.

Assuming they have sufficient bandwidth, if you are not considered a tier one client there is the significant risk you will not get assigned the best project resources they have at their disposal.

The true value of independence

Many businesses and vendors go into projects with the best of intentions and faith in their abilities to deliver them successfully, however having an intermediary in a customer-vendor relationship can be highly effective in ensuring a project doesn't get bogged down when things go wrong.

The independent project manager or system integrator will hold both parties to account to keep their end of the bargain and in return they will be responsible to both parties for delivering the scope of the project.

It is a release valve that can protect the outcome of the project and also protect the vendor/client relationship into the future.

Government v Private Projects: Are they more challenging?

What are the key characteristics that set Government projects apart from their private sector counterparts?

It is not uncommon for project managers to go through their entire career delivering projects exclusively in the private sector.

A project manager with strong project fundamentals should – theoretically – be able to deliver a project successfully in either sector, however many PMs will never give public sector projects serious consideration or they may be overlooked when competing with project managers who have prior Government project experience.

The delivery of projects in the public sector can be extremely nuanced. First time project managers can often be brought undone due to this lack of experience even if they are very experienced project managers in the private sector.

So is the delivery of public sector projects more challenging and if so, what are the key characteristics that set them apart from their private sector cousins?

No governance short cuts

Project governance is an essential component of any project. In the private sector, the level of governance 'imposed' upon a project can often be influenced by the organisation's project delivery maturity or, more often than not, the regular availability of senior executives to either attend steering committees etc. or focus on the project.

This can give rise to projects being delivered with a lighter touch of governance than was originally planned, giving the project manager certain freedoms.

Within the public sector, however, the governance structure and processes are more strictly adhered to from the senior executive down, including consistent attendance at meetings, approval processes, construction and timely delivery of reporting packs and so on.

This is especially true for the large programs. A project manager who does not get on top of the overall governance demands of the project and put in place and then follow the mandated procedures will quickly be found wanting.

The logistics will be challenging – always

It's critical that the project manager quickly comes to grips with the various processes required to run Government projects, such as:

- Approval processes for business cases, change requests etc.,
- How to on-board team members including the hiring;
- Sourcing space for teams;
- Procurement of basic equipment (desktops, phones, etc);
- The general procurement process; and
- Vendor management processes.

Within the private sector, there is often a significant amount of flexibility, particularly with delivering critical projects, when addressing the day-to-day needs of the project.

Within Government projects there is usually one correct path and few, if any, short cuts. Adding to the complexity, however, is that the correct path is often difficult to discern.

For a project manager to be successful, they need to either fully understand the correct procedures in detail or engage experienced team members, like coordinators, who have the required knowledge. The focus on project hygiene is critical to any project running smoothly; from the business case onwards through to delivery.

The upside – your funding won't be cut!

It's true: one of the upsides of the strict adherence to governance and processes within government projects is that, once in place, the funding for projects is protected to a far greater extent than within the private sector.

Whilst it may often be a longer and more complex route to funding approval, once in place, it is typically maintained throughout the duration of the project.

Unlike private sector projects, government project funding is less at the mercy of external impacts from management re-organisations, merger and acquisition activity, or senior executives changing their mind on priorities mid-project.

Risk management is not optional

Management of risk in a government project takes on new meaning and its influence can be seen throughout all aspects of the project.

Whether it's a lengthier sign-off process for funding or general approvals, regular internal assurance scrutiny, greater governance requirements or more rigorous testing – in terms of types of testing and depth – the management of risk is omnipresent for government projects.

A strong and sustained focus on risk management throughout the life cycle of the project is not optional for government projects if the project manager wants to be successful.

Straddling both worlds requires some essential modifications

The points above are not exhaustive but are a good snapshot of some of the key aspects of how government projects are different from their private enterprise cousins. Government projects may not be more challenging, but they are very nuanced and that requires a different approach.

Good project managers should still theoretically be able to straddle both worlds and be successful, but they will need to modify their way of working as required when moving into government projects, particularly if it is for the first time.

CHAPTER 11
WHEN IN DOUBT, PLAN

How do you know you are really on time?

Time management is probably the most challenging of the six competing constraints that project managers need to deal with.

Most projects have some form of project schedule. However the extent to which a project schedule can be relied upon is a function of many variables such as complexity, resource availability, external providers, key dependencies and even the way it was built and is maintained.

The reality of time

Time Management is probably the most challenging of the six competing constraints that project managers need to deal with.

Time expires at a regular and predictable rate, regardless of whether a team uses it effectively or not. This is a simple yet important concept to recognise, as all project activities are bound by time and project feasibility is typically based upon assumptions for on-time delivery.

With this in mind in order to minimise the scheduling risk , consideration should be given to engaging a specialist scheduler to drive this process for complex projects and programs.

When to engage a Master Scheduler

A Master Scheduler's role complements the Project Manager's role by providing specialist control over the most complex process in project management.

This role is particularly important when there are multiple streams of work with interdependencies, which by their nature cannot rely upon a project manager's intuition regarding delivery.

To give a project the best chance of success, it is important that the schedule describes a realistic path to delivery. This means catering for the approved scope, cost, time, resources, and change requests, within agreed levels of risk and quality.

A well-constructed schedule, coupled with diligent and disciplined project updates, can provide a level of certainty and support effective communication

Not only does a Master Scheduler produce a baseline schedule but they also construct it in a manner that readily supports "What if...?" scenario planning. This allows the project manager to pro-actively plan for the inevitable change in a project .

When should a schedule be reviewed?

It is important that the schedule is generated correctly during the planning phase and then kept up to date to reflect any changes occurring in the project.

External schedule reviews can help ensure the accuracy of the project schedule and should be executed at the beginning of the project and at key milestones or during major re-planning exercises.

A schedule review applying a formalised best practice approach can quickly assess the veracity of a schedule and present a series of actions, which if implemented, will improve the schedule's reliability and present greater certainty for stakeholders.

Such a review should identify areas for improvement, suggested approaches to apply improvements, benefits of applying the improvements, and key schedule risks that the project team would need to manage, in the absence of improvement.

This schedule review process will help drive quality into project schedules but does not replace the need for project managers and schedulers to continue to maintain their schedules on a regular basis to ensure they remain accurate and achievable.

When art meets science: planning and scheduling

To get a true and accurate picture of a project's delivery timeline the planning and scheduling function must work in concert.

While planning may be viewed as an art and scheduling as a science, it's the way art and science meet that enables a high level of certainty in project delivery.

And though planning and scheduling have many similarities, they are distinctly different functions in project management.

Planning as Art

Project planning is a team effort, involving many stakeholders at distinct times of the planning process providing a variety of inputs. Initial planning may involve skilled executives to determine the worthiness of an investment and the planned benefits this investment will realise.

Design planning may involve solution architects that provide solution options for teams to consider. Requirements gathering may involve a number of specialists, skilled in their ability to understand what the key business stakeholders require.

Decision-making is key to effective planning. The team needs to determine an overall delivery strategy, that lends itself to effective control and performance management in areas as diverse as scope, risk, communications, cost, quality and time.

The art is in bringing together these key people and their areas of expertise to develop a robust plan for successful project delivery.

Scheduling as Science

Project scheduling however can be best described as a science focused on time management.

A project scheduler takes the output and decisions from the various planning processes and uses this as input to scheduling processes. For instance, the project scope will have deliverables with defined activities set in a particular sequence.

Each of the activities will require certain resources to do the work. The type of resource will determine the number of work periods required to complete the work and provide the basis for developing baseline, and as-built schedule models.

So what tools and techniques does a project manager have at their disposal to integrate planning art with scheduling science?

The Work Breakdown Structure (WBS) and WBS Dictionary

In simple terms, the work breakdown structure (WBS) describes the project scope as a set of deliverables arranged in a hierarchy. The WBS Dictionary describes each of the deliverables in greater detail.

These details would typically include a WBS Level, WBS Code, Definition, schedule activities, resources, resource estimations, planned duration to complete the deliverable, and a deliverable owner.

Armed with this information, a project scheduler has information at an appropriate level that reflects the degree of certainty the project team has at a particular point in time.

The team may be only able to describe next phase deliverables with a high level of certainty.

For future deliverables, the level of certainty will improve over time, as better information becomes available, providing the basis for replanting the work remaining, updating the WBS dictionary, and modifying the project schedule.

The net benefit of balancing the art and science

Effective planning sets the overall direction of the project. Robust schedules then provide clear direction, so teams work on the right activities at the right time and are focused on what's required to achieve the outcomes for on-time delivery.

By providing a project structure and environment where planning and scheduling co-exist it promotes good project delivery and enables the stakeholders to objectively measure cost and delivery performance.

Assessing performance from the baseline

A project baseline provides an essential starting point for monitoring and assessing the performance of your projects.

Without it, your team – and business as a whole – has no reference to measure against either during the roll out of your projects or when post-implementation reviews are undertaken.

What does a baseline provide?

A baseline is a planned state, describing what the business expects the project to look like throughout its development, and typically includes:

- Planned start and finish dates
- Planned effort, which may be shown in hours against resources
- Budgeted or planned cost
- Budgeted or planned revenue

That said, "baseline" can mean different things to different stakeholders and can be expressed in different ways.

For example, as a result of planning processes and expected output, the following baselines are typical interpretations:

- Scope baseline
- Cost performance baseline
- Schedule performance baseline
- Technical baseline
- Product baseline
- Cash baseline
- Benefits realisation baseline

These baselines enable the project manager to use baseline types that may describe and communicate project delivery information in different ways to meet the needs and information requirements of various stakeholders in a project. However, when measuring performance overall, the Performance Measurement Baseline becomes critical.

What is the Performance Measurement Baseline (PMB)?

The Performance Measurement Baseline (PMB) is a time-based budget plan that outlines how the project will be completed and against which performance measures it will be evaluated. The PMB is a direct output of the project planning process; planning typically involves all known stakeholders that have an interest in a project's outcome.

A PMB is not a single baseline schedule, but rather is made up of several baselines that describe the approved scope, cost and time. The risks are embedded in the PMB and are quantified in the contingencies.

For example:

Baseline type	Documentation	Purpose
Scope Baseline	• Scope Statement • Work Breakdown Structure • Work Breakdown Structure Dictionary	The scope baseline outlines the requirements for the scope of the project and how the work will be broken down.
Cost Performance Baseline	• Resource estimates • Cost Management Plan • Budget development, including provisions for risk	This is a version of the budget, used to compare actual expenditures with planned expenditures, over time.

Schedule Performance Baseline	Project schedule	This is a specific version of the schedule, used to compare actual delivery to planned delivery.

These baselines are vital for evaluating performance during the project to judge whether the project is on track, as well as enable project teams to re-assess scheduling throughout a project development.

What benefit can a PMB provide for stakeholders?

The key question for many stakeholders is "... what did we accomplish for the effort we applied?".

By applying diligence in the planning processes and developing these specific baseline types, the project manager can objectively assess progress using Earned Value Management tools.

Earned Value (EV) metrics provide the answers to the question above by showing the effort, costs and time involved in a project, an integrated viewpoint that is driven by the PMB.

By applying diligence in the planning processes and developing these specific baseline types, the project manager may use Earned Value Management tools to objectively gauge progress.

Earned Value Management techniques are valuable for large or complex projects and we'll explore these in more detail in a future bulletin article.

What if we need to change the baseline?

The most appropriate time to consider re-base lining a schedule is when there are approved changes to scope, time, cost and risk that will likely impact the baseline delivery date.

This approach also means that other issues such as scope creep, poor execution by inexperienced resources, poor planning, or poor change control are not triggers for reassessing the baseline.

However, if the problems are a reflection of built-in overruns caused by bad estimates, then the remaining work requires re-planning, the estimates require revision, and the schedule will need re-baselining.

Better, quicker, cheaper projects – it is possible

With the increasing pressure for business to be dynamic most organisations are struggling with how to get projects completed cheaper, faster and without comprising quality.

This article presents one approach that can be considered to address this dilemma.

A dynamic, evolving environment

The dramatic advancements in technology, even over the past 10 years, have created a business environment now where two things are clear:

- **Change** – the pace of change and the need for a business to be dynamic is at levels never experienced before
- **Connectivity** – the maturity of technology has enabled almost any application, device and location to connected and interconnected
- This evolution has real implications for project implementation:
- **No longer can projects take years to complete.** Business is changing too fast and long-term projects will not often make the ROIs they set out to as technology and business requirements have changed (often multiple times) before the project delivers
- **Many components of end to end business processes are now outsourced** (BPO), or acquired as a service (SaaS) and not developed or managed in-house

The technology leaders have stood up to this challenge by seeking to build out enterprise reference architectures that allow for projects to deliver quickly, autonomously and yet by adhering to the enterprise architecture work seamlessly together.

So how do we then leverage this change to do projects better, faster and cheaper? The answer we call "Hypothesis" based implementation.

How does a hypothesis implementation work?

A hypothesis implementation goes like this:

"Based upon some key criteria we believe this is the best solution and then going about proving we are right" – in other words ruling the solution out rather than ruling one in.

Some criteria considered in devising the hypothesis could include industry research (like the Gartner Magic Quadrant), knowledge of specifics for the business, and the current and future business strategies and of course the enterprise architecture standards of the organisation.

A Project might go something like this:

- **Capture high-level requirements** from a small, senior, stakeholder group
- Triage and prioritize requirements – draw a line under the requirements that deliver 80% of the value sought using a correlation of priority, capability gap and business benefit
- **Investigate and create a high level solution** using by applying the key criteria (end to end People, Process and Technology components)
- Select the Product/s that best fits
- **Get going** – Prove the Concept and iterate

The hypothetical project approach is more about ruling out a solution than ruling it in. It makes allowance for high-level requirements but does not get laboured in detailed requirements.

In most cases solutions will leverage the cloud (IaaS, PaaS, SaaS) over in house infrastructure and application development.

The only constant in business is change

This approach recognises the principle that the only constant in business is change and that time is definitely of the essence.

By leveraging the work of experts, applying enterprise standards and procuring components of the solution as a service, businesses can rapidly deploy solutions of high quality and low cost and low risk.

CHAPTER 12

STRATEGY & ARCHITECTURE: KEY ENABLERS TO SUCCESS

Pilot v Production - Architecture red flags?

Pilot programs often fast track new technology into an organisation, however is "just enough" architecture the right approach to take into a full-scale implementation?

Pilot deployment is often a fast-tracked way of getting new technology introduced into an organisation, usually within a particular department or business unit.

The intent is to leverage the success of the pilot to deploy into a full-scale implementation.

Successfully delivering the pilot can provide a strong argument for "just enough" architecture to ensure that the technology works within the business environment and adheres to enterprise standards and reference architecture.

The question, however, is whether this is enough to take it to full implementation?

Start out as you mean to continue

Quay's experience has shown that when more consideration is given to better architecture from the outset, the results are also better. It's important to identify potential red flags from the outset and some of the considerations may include:

Risk and Reward trade-offs between rapid deployment using a systems led approach (vanilla COTS) versus "a business change approach" which considers specific business requirements, business change capacity and involves defining the business led logical transition steps.

Guiding Principles to assist in project and architecture decision making. For example having principles which will influence whether functional gaps will be addressed via customisation or business workarounds

Data and Information Architecture including data migration, data quality and data ownership including Master Data Management

Consideration and management of all aspects of the Architecture – Integration, Technology and Applications both pre and post production including often forgotten items such as Error Handling Frameworks, Change & Release Management, Technical and Functional support, Capacity Planning ,"end to end" business process performance and SLAs.

Operational impacts not just for implementation but also for ongoing support – skills, capacity etc

Plan early to get better outcomes

As with projects in general, the more time spent planning architecture from the outset, the better outcomes will be.

Don't fall into the trap that because it is a commercial off-the-shelf (COTS) deployment that the proper application of architecture principles and practices is less important.

Driving business value into the technology roadmap

Technology is one of the key enablers of any business and when it is aligned with the core business – regardless of sector – it is a significant competitive advantage.

Technology enables scalability, agility and constant availability, however when it is not aligned or not delivered as required, its value becomes diminished and can reduce the capability of a business to be successful.

In the absence of an aligned roadmap to the business, providers and supporters of technology risk being regarded as a hindrance rather than a strategic enabler, increasing the likelihood that the business may consider outsourcing IT.

The growth of cloud-based services is a tantalising carrot for businesses that see misalignment between its core business and IT delivery.

So how can IT show genuine leadership and value to their organisation when delivering technology that supports and runs the business? We've outlined below a quick guide to successfully engaging and understanding the business to build an aligned, valued technology strategy.

Understand the business

At the highest level, IT needs to understand what the purpose of the business is, as well as the core business. Why is the organisation in business, where is it going and who does it serve?

Understanding and documenting IT's understanding of these fundamentals may require a review of the business's strategy, engaging in dialogue with users within the organisation and developing a robust understanding of the end user's needs.

IT must understand the critical business functions required to support delivery of the core business. Exercises that can facilitate and quantify this level of understanding include:

- Business capability modelling
- High-level business process mapping
- Pain points analysis
- Defining what success looks like for the business in 12-24 months' time.

The purpose of these exercises is to develop a documented understanding of the business, where it is going and assessing its current and future technology needs.

Translate business understanding into IT understanding

It often becomes apparent from these types of exercises that not only is technology not supporting the business but also that the culture between business and IT is not aligned.

Analyse the gaps in applications, information infrastructure, leadership and organisational structure to see where technology supports and fails in the business.

With a documented understanding of business and end customer needs, IT has the opportunity to develop a better perspective on how business capability and processes influence technology and the departments that deliver and support it.

Develop a 'future state'

Once the gaps from technology and culture are understood then the future IT and technology state can be defined.

This enables a clear demarcation between the current and future technology needs alongside the level of service and support required by IT to be of value and beneficial to the business.

Aligning application, information and infrastructure states with future organisational structure(s) and capability requirements support and enable the business is a formula for success.

The roadmap for change

A technology roadmap is essential to ensure that short-term and long-term goals are articulated in clear stages that show how the business will get to the ideal future state, mapped out as a sequence of activities that generate value to the business.

The entire organisation should be represented in the construction of the roadmap to ensure that programs of activities are aligned with business needs and priorities.

Program of works

Guidance and governance should be established around programs of work to deliver packages within each program.

This program of works should consist of a list of dimensioned projects from within the roadmap, referencing defined criteria such as:

- Time
- Cost
- Complexity
- Business benefit
- Risks & issues
- Other relevant attributes

The roadmap and the program of works should be living breathing documents that are reassessed regularly to ensure relevance and continued benefit.

Drive genuine value though engagement and alignment

IT can drive genuine value when it understands and defines what the real value of a product and service is to the business (end customer).

Building an aligned roadmap is most effective when the end customers are part of the process, because it allows IT to ensure that delivery and support of technology is aligned to the current and future needs of the organisation; to deliver key business enabling technology tools; and remain a strategic enabler rather than a hindrance to business success.

The 5 benefits of a Capability Model

Business can be perceived to be quite complex,
especially when approached from the bottom up.

One mistake that can be made when attempting to understand how IT aligns to the business is to dive prematurely into the detail, without first taking a look at what the business looks like and really does from 30,000 feet.

In recent editions of the Quay Bulletin, we've outlined the benefits of aligning IT strategically with the business and highlighting the need for IT to understand the critical business functions required to support delivery of core business to be seen as a business enabler.

Building on that discussion, one of the most important attributes of demonstrating good understanding of the business is to distil the complexity into simple high-level themes. These themes can provide the basis for discussion and decision making without the need to explain complex operations.

A single 'placemat' view of the business provides this simplicity and enables constructive conversations at all levels from operational management through to the company executives.

So how do you get this single page view?

What is Capability Modelling?

In Quay's experience, we've found that one of the best ways to achieve both the placemat view and demonstrate an understanding of the business is to model its capabilities.

Mapping out the building blocks that form the stable business functions within the organisation provides a great lens through which to view that high level understanding of what the business actually does. It's an exercise that can provide great value. We see there are five key benefits of capability modelling:

1. Identify gaps and duplications

A model of the business enables both the business and IT to quickly see where gaps and duplications exist in the current state across a range of services such as:

- Applications (Software)
- Information (Business, corporate, organisational and operational data)
- Infrastructure (Hardware, network services, servers, capacity etc.)
- People (Organisational structure, process, capability etc)

When planning for the future, this model provides a roadmap for projects and portfolios of work that IT can deliver to support business growth. CIOs and CTO's can then have informed discussions with the business and IT teams alike using this easily understood model as the centre piece for decision making. Identifying duplicated applications and services also provide opportunities for cost reduction through consolidation and centralisation.

2. Clearly articulate business pain points and achieve quick wins

The model enables IT to have the conversation with the business and objectively determine the pain points experienced by the business from the perspective of the business (not IT's version of events).

These pain points are great opportunities to deliver focused quick wins especially in the delivery of services to the business. Focusing on these pain points demonstrates to the business that IT has the ability to address the issues that are important in a business context.

3. Prioritise and focus projects against strategy and real need

The model enables the organisation to review all proposed initiatives to see if they will actually address the pain points and gaps. Doing less but doing it better and ensuring it has the right impact is important for successful outcomes and this process ensures that the money is being spent where it is most needed.

4. A communication tool

Steps 1 to 3 facilitate a clear communication tool that IT can use to demonstrate that they know what is important to the business and ensure communication of technology initiatives is done utilising language that the business will understand.

5. Grows with the business

The model is a representation of the business at any point in time and provides a current view of how IT is delivering services to the business. By keeping it up to date it becomes the essential communication piece across the business.

Capability models as an essential tool

Capability models are not a 'nice to have' but should be seen as an essential tool for any business.

They will provide significant benefit for IT to better understand the context of the business it is supporting. Equally as powerful is the tools ability to demonstrate to the business that IT can be a key enabler and a partner. And anything that brings the business and IT together to solve common problems using a common language should be strongly considered as a 'must have' for all organisations.

The role of architecture in successful project outcomes

What are the three main tangible benefits that enterprise architecture can deliver to a business project?

Enterprise architecture provides a set of tools that help organisations to align their strategic objectives with operational consequences and IT decision-making, however it is not only an IT tool.

It is a business instrument that also aligns the organisation at all levels with its business objectives.

The 'perfect world' alignment of enterprise architecture and project delivery

In a perfect world, enterprise architecture and project delivery should always have strong alignment, which is critical to building and deploying projects that meet the long-term vision and strategy of the business. Often projects will be run in silos, or focused on a tactical outcome without considering the wider organisation. Strong Enterprise Architecture can help avoid this happening. Here's how:

Business architects create business models based on the emerging business vision and strategy from the executive leadership team.

The business models form the basis for future business requirements for information, processing, security and integration solutions. Information, application, security and technology architects each design the required systems – initially at a strategic level – to guide portfolio planning and later provide detailed solutions to support individual implementation projects.

Portfolio Managers then use the models to devise programs consisting of smaller projects via a roadmap to attain the target Enterprise Architecture. Individual projects are then implemented, each tackling a piece of the transformation puzzle.

These Enterprise Architecture frameworks will drive clear scope and requirements for technology projects that are targeted to outcomes (tactical and strategic) across all levels of the business.

Three tangible benefits of strong enterprise architecture

There are benefits beyond sound project outcomes that enterprise architecture will achieve, for example:

1. Cost Management

Enterprise Architecture can provide clarity and targeted frameworks across a range of elements to capture costs, including:

- Total cost of operation of the application(s).
- Costs of infrastructure, hardware, software and networks.
- Development costs if software is needed.
- Cost of business operations once transition over from the project.

2. Risk Management

Enterprise Architecture can help manage risk in:

- Non-compliance (i.e. regulatory / legal).
- Excessive project costs (well defined outcomes and design minimise cost blow-out)
- Loss of intellectual property (retained in-house).

3. Business Agility

Companies focused on business agility and flexibility with well set-up Enterprise Architecture can improve flexibility through:

- Better decision-making support, thanks to greater awareness of the business outcomes and what the project needs to achieve.
- Faster realisation of new business processes that are aligned to outcomes.

- Improved flexibility to outsource non-core activities with a deeper understanding of what core business capability is as well as what can be outsourced.

Right projects at the right time

When a project is in scoping and requirements phase, a robust Enterprise Architecture can ensure that costs, risks, business outcomes and agility are controlled through deep insights and clearly defined roadmaps.

Clearly defined frameworks and a thorough understanding of what the business needs to achieve a fit for purpose Enterprise Architecture provides organisations tools and a governance capability that helps ensure they are focused on the 'right projects at the right time'.

This remains a critical component to sound portfolio management and overall successful project delivery across an organisation.

The case for a DAM strategy

If you were to take a moment and think about how many different places that digital assets can exist within your organisation, it's easy to see that there are risks and opportunities for how they are managed.

As businesses increasingly focus on interaction with their customers in a digital world, your organisation's ability to organise, manage, use and re-use digital assets is taking on increasing importance due to the volume, complexity and fragmentation of those assets across different storage places and devices.

But what is a 'digital asset' and why are they now so important to an organisations on-going digital strategy?

Digital assets – what are they?

Digital assets include the multitude of electronic files that a business may develop, acquire or buy, for example:

- Product images
- Photographs
- Video files
- Audio files
- Presentations
- Logos, design files and other brand assets

These digital assets have the potential to be used and reused within your business and would cost time, money and energy to replace or re-create if lost, corrupted or inaccessible.

Take a moment to think about how many different places digital asses might exist in your organisation: network drives, local computer hard drives, memory sticks, cloud drives (personal and business), mobile devices and so on. Then imagine how hard it would be to identify and access them when you don't really know what lives where.

Digital Asset Management requires a DAM strategy

Digital Asset Management (DAM) is important for two simple reasons: time and money. Right now, more than ever before, marketing is driving a real-time customer experience underpinned by the use of digital assets.

Marketing departments are being given increased budgets to spend directly on digital marketing, resulting in a significant increase in the creation and use of these assets.

As time-to-market rates drop rapidly, the ability to leverage digital assets efficiently is becoming a critical business enabler.

Those businesses that cannot readily identify and manage their digital assets will struggle to compete against those that can.

Digital Asset Management (DAM) provides the tools and techniques that manage the ingestion, annotation, cataloguing, storage, retrieval and distribution of your digital assets, which substantially improves your marketing team's ability to maximise and leverage on a recurring basis.

When done effectively, digital assets can be stored, identified and accessed quickly ensuring the greatest return for the business rather than re-inventing the wheel.

Furthermore, where some of your digital assets are licensed from a third party, DAM provides a structured approach to ensuring the digital rights obligations attached to those assets are appropriately and accurately fulfilled, preventing any unexpected surprises later on.

The critical issue in Digital Asset Management

The major issue with many businesses today is that they have no DAM strategy. Digital assets have been acquired or created without any coordinated approach resulting in an inability to identify what they are, where they are and how to use them effectively.

In fact, in many cases there is actually no comprehension of what digital assets are and the role they play for an organisation.

This is highly inefficient and will eventually erode the business's competitiveness where speed and turnaround is of high value. Hunting for assets or recreating them is a hugely inefficient and costly exercise.

The lack of a standardised approach can also lead to version control (quality) and third party licensing (liability) issues, not to mention the cost of storing duplicated assets.

Discovering your digital assets

The first step in managing digital assets is to understand exactly what digital assets your organisation has.

Undertaking a structured review to identify the type and location of your digital assets and then cataloguing them allows you to see the type, volume and locations of what you have.

The next step is to build a DAM strategy that details the manner in which:

- Digital assets are created (or acquired)
- How and where they will be stored, how they will be identified,
- How they can be searched for and retrieved and
- Any policies that apply to them (e.g. third party rights, version control etc.).

Once you have your strategy, a Gap Analysis between current and desired state should be undertaken and a plan built to address the gaps. In many cases leveraging a Digital Asset Management Software (DAMS) product might form a part of the desired state.

DAMS come pre-built with the ability to apply business logic and often a high degree of automation as to how assets are ingested, centrally stored, described, retrieved and with policies to govern them (often workflow capabilities are a key enabler for this).

The next step is to execute your plan and transform your organisation to ensure that Digital Asset Management is a competitive advantage – not a disadvantage.

Let us help you regain control of your digital

If you have lost control of your digital profile or it is underutilised, Quay Consulting can help bring some order and sanity back. We have extensive experience working in media, developing suitable processes and engaging highly experienced consultants with deep experience in the digital asset domain.

Quay can work with your team to undertake a structured approach to digital asset identification, build a Digital Asset Management Strategy (including business and IT architecture and product evaluation) and help deliver a digital outcome that keeps your organisation ahead of the competition.

How to Make Technology Enable Business Strategy in Ever Changing Times

How can we make sure that our IT capability supports the business effectively during significant transformation?

Beyond death and taxes there is another constant in the universe called change.

Right now business globally is undergoing significant transformation in response to the risks, issues and opportunities presented through the global financial crisis. IT more than ever before is a critical enabler of that change; so how do we make sure our IT capability supports the business effectively?

Lens shift: supporting business capability

The answer to this question can be challenging, as often the business strategy is either a work in progress, not agreed or simply reactive to change.

Without this baseline to reference against how can IT effectively support what the business needs? The answer is to shift the lens from enabling business strategy to supporting business capability.

A business capability defines the organisation's capacity to successfully perform a unique business activity.

A Business Capability Model is the top layer of the business architecture distilling onto a page what the business does or needs to do to meet its objectives, which represents:

- The building blocks of the business
- Stable business functions which are unique and independent from each other

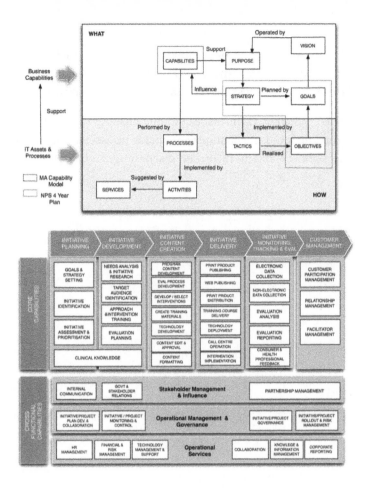

This snapshot of capabilities is extremely powerful in helping shape the organisation and is invaluable in driving out the supporting IT Technology, Information and Applications required.

Assess current capability against required capability

By undertaking an assessment of current capability against required capability IT can then define its roadmap in the context of the business needs and put it back on the business to prioritise which capability gaps need to be addressed in what order.

Taking the example above by simply colour coding each capability Red, Amber, Green with respect to the current state against required state IT can have a business driven conversation as to priorities.

Furthermore, when a business capability changes (less often than strategy) the impact of the change can quickly be assessed against both the business and IT and an informed discussion can be held.

About Quay Consulting

Quay Consulting is a professional services business operating in the project management landscape, transforming strategy into fit-for-purpose project delivery.

Established in 2006, Quay has achieved sustained growth by providing our clients with real-world, relevant knowledge to help create project delivery environments aligned to their capability and specific project demands.

Quay Consulting is proud to have been included on the BRW's Fast 100 growth companies for three consecutive years in 2011, 2012 and 2013, which is testament to the continued success of our model and our ability to successfully support and service our clients over a sustained period of time.

Contact Us

Quay Consulting Pty Ltd

Level 9, 19-31 Pitt Street

Sydney NSW 2000

Phone: 02 9098 6300

Follow Us

Quay Bulletin - http://www.quayconsulting.com.au

LinkedIn - https://www.linkedin.com/company/quay-consulting

Twitter - https://twitter.com/quayconsulting

End Notes

[i] Tzu, S., Zi, S. and Giles, L. (2006) *The art of war.* United States: Filiquarian Publishing.

[ii] *Prosci Benchmarking Report* (2011) Available at: http://www.change-management.com/best-practices-report.htm (Accessed: 17 September 2013).

[iii] *The State of Big Data Infrastructure Management Benchmarking Global Big Data Users to Drive Future Performance - CA Technologies* (2015) Available at: https://www.ca.com/us/register/forms/collateral/the-state-of-big-data-infrastructure.aspx (Accessed: 17 June 2015).

[iv] Ward, J., Daniel, E. and Peppard, J. (2007) 'Building Better Business Cases for IT Investments', *California Management Review*, .